MW01136802

Something Good for a Change

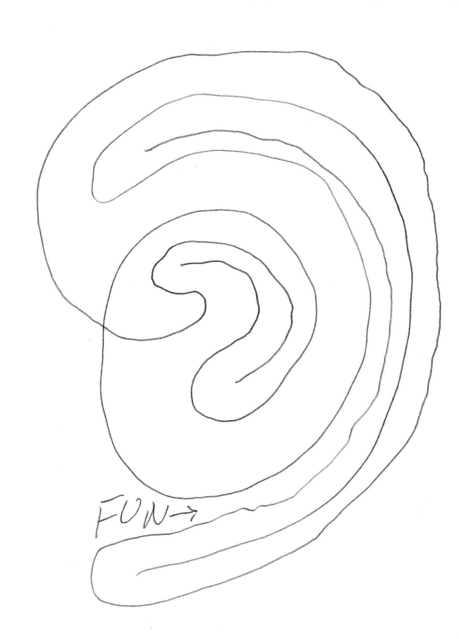

FUN→

Something Good for a Change

Random Notes on Peace Thru Living

Wavy Gravy

St. Martin's Press, New York

Design by Jaye Zimet

Library of Congress Cataloging-in-Publication Data
Wavy Gravy.
      Something good for a change : random notes on peace thru living / Wavy Gravy.
         p. cm.
     ISBN 0-312-07838-2
      1. Wavy Gravy. 2. Social reformers—United States—Biography. 3. Radicals—United States—Biography. 4. Voluntarism—United States. 5. Charities—United States.   I. Title.
    HV28.W38A3   1992
    361.7'4'092—dc20
    [B]   92-1096
                                        CIP

10 9 8 7 6 5 4 3 2

For our children's children

Contents

ACKNOWLEDGMENTS   ix

SOMETHING GOOD FOR A CHANGE   xi

TOWARD THE FUN   3

WOODSTOCK, THE FIRST HUNDRED YEARS   12

THE HOG FARM TODAY   22

PEANUTS IN MY HAMBURGER   27

PICK A NOSE   31

APEX WITH SEVA   35

MY FAN   43

REFLECTIONS ON ASCENSION TO FLAVOR-
HOOD   47

THE CLOWN BY A NOSE   51

THE MUSE IS LOOSE   55

HOT SMELLY WATER   59

ME AND MARGARET MEAD   63

WHAT MAKES WAVY RUN   67

THE PSYCHEDELIC SOLUTION   76

CONFESSIONS OF A MUTANT DOVE   80

TOOTH OR CONSEQUENCES   90

HOW I PASSED THE ACID TEST   93

JANIS'S LAST LAUGH   99

IT ONLY HURTS WHEN I DON'T LAUGH   102

A PIECE ON GARBAGE   107

FOR WHOM THE TOLL KNOLLS   113

REX, THE WONDER DOG   117
FEAR ITSELF   122
I LOVE PARIS IN THE HOSPITAL   125
SACRED PLACES   130
WHAT'S IN A NAME?   134
TRUNGPA   137
SANTA   140
WINNARAINBOW   146
FROM THE RIDICULOUS TO THE SUBLIME   156
KATE WOLF'S MYLAR RAINBOW WIG   160
EARTH PEOPLE'S PARK   164
ABBIE HOFFMAN WITHOUT TEARS   172
THAT'S THE BAG I'M IN   176
THE GARDEN CLUB   179
THE SACRED SHIT LIST   187
AM I EXPERIENCED?   191
THE FIRST CHURCH OF FUN   194
BUBBLES ARE FOREVER   199
MY SEAMY UNDERBELLY   202
HEALTH ANGELS   207
BASIC HUMAN NEEDS   212
DEAD CENTER   217
SIGH ALONG WITH MITCH   223
A QUICK SKETCH OF MY THUMBNAIL   227
EARLY EINSTEIN   233
BYE BYE BILL   236
ALWAYS PUT YOUR GOOD WHERE IT WILL
    DO THE MOST   241

Acknowledgments

I should like to thank Joel Makower at Tilden Press for his endless prodding and invaluable suggestions. It was Joel who brought my life and vision to Jim Fitzgerald of St. Martin's Press, the most patient of editors.

This book took its physical form in a series of hideouts and sanctuaries provided by friends like Cedar, the Brilliants, and Peter and Marsha.

Last, I should like to thank my wife Jahanara for helping to dispel my unreasonable suspicion and fear of the computer that has served me so well in the final edit.

Something Good for a Change

You have some Gravy on your eyes. This is Wavy Gravy—author, kid's camp director, humanitarian, activist, pacifist, clown, and temple of accumulated error. I currently reside within these very words you're looking at right now. Just gaze directly at the page. Start to open your eyes really wide, WIDER STILL! Just explode your eyeballs onto the page.

SEE ALL THE WORDS AT ONCE.

LET YOURSELF BEGIN TO FLOAT IN LIGHT.

NOW! Quick, touch my cape!

Go WHOOSH . . . and

SQUEEZE YOUR EYES SHUT! See those bright spots on your eyelids? Now go for the light inside the center of your head. Head for the blinding flashes. Those are my major true-life experiences reduced to a series of random slides awaiting reactualization in the carousel of my mind.

SOOOooo, let's give the whole thing a flip or a spin. The beginning of the book has absolutely nothing to do with the chronology of my life, but is merely my own personal running order of the moment (if I were Mr. Random). But don't let me intimidate you!

FEEL FREE TO FLIP OR SPIN.

Now go WHOOSH

and begin.

Could We Have the Next Slide, Please?

Toward the Fun

Toward the fun is a spiritual pun on the sacred sentence of the Sufis, "Toward the One." It is also the motto of Wavy Gravy and Camp Winnarainbow. That's me, and the kids' camp I helped to found over fifteen years ago. I am also a founder of The First Church of Fun, whose formal rites are practiced only on the first of April. One would think I'd have a pretty good bead on this fun stuff by now. One would think wrong.

Wavy Gravy says, "Thinking gets in the way of thought."

"What the duck duck does that mean?"

Exactly: a pair of ducks.

What that means is putting things together that don't make sense.

Nonsense!

Exactly! But you must go beyond Nonsense to achieve the Zen state I call NO sense and enter the frontiers of Fun. For instance, take the Nobody for President campaign slogan, "If Nobody wins, Nobody loses!"

Did you feel the center of your head do a little flip-flop?

I certainly did the first time I said it. I found that sensation both liberating and silly. I also found it funny, which Webster's Elementary Dictionary says is an adjective that causes laughter, and which further suggests that laughter is the sound of laughing, and laugh is a verb meaning to show amusement, mirth, and joy by smiling or chuckling, etc. Are we having fun yet?

You betcha! Laughter is the audio announcement that Fun is being had. In its fullest form laughter is both healthy and holy. The dictionary further suggests that to amuse means to "delight a person's sense of humor."

Wavy Gravy says, "If you don't have a sense of humor it just isn't funny any more."

Did I get you that time? At least a little flip? Don't worry if you didn't flop yet. Just keep on flipping away and the flop will come. In fact it is that moment between the flip and the flop that the major insights and healing occur.

Try vocalizing the flip as "Aaahhhhhhhhh." Imagine the Angel of Comedy inserting an invisible tongue depressor into your head—*Aaahhhhhh*—till you are wide open and totally relaxed. Enter the heavenly hyphen (-), followed by the *great* release: "HA!" All together now! AH-HA! Again. AH-HA! Once more. AH-HA! I think you got it. Now, go with the flop: HA HA HA HA HA HA.

What goes HA HA PLOP HA HA PLOP?

If you said two people laughing their heads off you have just initiated yourself into the Order of the Loose Wig.

If you said, "an amusing bowel movement" (without thinking), you also enter the Order.

BUT if you said the more advanced, "I give up," you are momentarily out of order and must return to the state of "Aaahhhhhhhh" and tell me what the chicken said when she laid the square egg.

If you did not answer, "Ouch! that hurt!" you qualify as a hard case and must again activate your inner "Aaahhhh" while you seek out the true-life experience that I call the "Train Wreck of the Mind" or flop-flip!

No two TWMs are alike. But they are easy to recognize and are BIG FUN! Here are a few of my own personal favorites to get you on the right track. These are extreme examples of tap dancing on the edge of fun and should not be practiced at home without a net. Here's the first.

All aboard! *Toot Toot Toot Choo Choo Choo I stink I'm tan I stink I'm a Clam choo choo HISSSSS*—followed by a great blast of steam from the ascending Locomotive of Fun. The steam is everywhere. Now the steam changes and becomes fog: thick yet shimmering with its own inner light on the cool California coast.

That's me standing with a few old friends appraising the moment. We are standing squarely in the center of the sixties and assessing the cosmos. Each of us asking our higher selves that colorful, kooky California kind of question: Are we about to fall into the Pacific Ocean or is Edgar Casey full of shit?

You can hear the waves pounding the cliffs of Tory Pines (although the fog covers everything like a giant leg warmer). All is muffled and spooky. The silence swallows both the traffic from Route One and the never-ending squawking of the seagulls. Only the pounding waves and the luminous fog and us hippies. Simultaneously, we sensed the possibility of impending doom, jumped in our jalopy, and lit out for Arizona.

It's pedal to the metal all the way to Barstow, where we pause for fuel and phone calls. Most Californians have either given or received one of these calls . . . usually in the dead of night:

"Hello John. Look, I know it's four in the morning but you're like my brother, man, and I just have to warn you about the earthquake. That's right! California is about to break off the edge of the United States and fall into the Pacific Ocean. Phoenix could be the next San Diego. I gotta talk fast. It could happen any minute. It's in all the prophesies. There hasn't been a planetary alignment like this in all of recorded history. The magnetic pull . . . of . . .

"What do you mean, Am I tripping? Well up yours, asshole. Listen, there isn't much time. You had better get your ass on an airplane and tell all your friends cuz we're outta here. Good-bye. I love you, man."

And it's blast outta Barstow and head for the Hopis. It is written in the Book of the Hopi that in a condition of planetary emergency the people of all races would gather together on the main mesa and await instructions from the spirit world.

We drove the desert deep into the Arizona dawn, and finally folded in a cheap motel and slept till the following afternoon. When we woke up, California was still firmly attached to the free world, so we knocked back a late lunch and set off for Old Oraibi in the center of Hopi land.

As our doom seemed a little less impending, we decided to take a little side trip to this out-of-the-way cliff dwelling we had heard about and make some music for the sunset. When we pulled up, the sun was splashing red and orange all over those burnt-sienna cliffs. Our flute sounds echoed endlessly amidst the ancient architecture. We shook our rattles and sang and prayed to the sunset. I shook with my right and explored with my left. I couldn't help it. There is something in me that just loves to root around in old-time stuff. So I'm praying away and looking under various rocks for something amazing, while the sun is settin' and the flutes are flutin' and I'm rootin'—when I freeze.

What's this I found? It was under that last rock. "Everybody, look!" All eyes turned, and there, illuminated in my shaking hand, was a very old slab of sandstone. On that stone was etched a sacred serpent. We all gasped in amazement as the snake in the stone turned blood red in the fading sun.

By chance I turned it over, and carved on the other side was "Made in Japan."

FLIP—and our skulls burst open to admit the locomotive and the rainbow and the cloud. How much time expired before the FLOP was anybody's guess. Then we bowed our heads and honored the creative genius who carefully carved and placed that stone in the devious hands of divine coincidence. It's been said that coincidence is a miracle that God doesn't take credit for. Coincidence is often the switchman in the train wreck of the mind.

Example number two is a bit less esoteric, as it happened in Berkeley on my fiftieth birthday and was fashioned by family and friends who arranged for my mind to go bye-bye—in full view of over three thousand people in the Berkeley Community Theater.

We called the show "The Wavy Gravy Fiftieth Birthday Benefit for Just about Everything" and afterwards I got to give away fifty thousand dollars to my favorite causes, like the Seva Foundation and the peace, homeless, and environmental movements. It was the perfect perk to honor my first half-century.

Jerry Garcia was scheduled to kick off but his bass player, Captain John Kahn, was lost in the ozone that stretches from Marin County to the East Bay. Jorma Kaukonen just happened to be in the area so he heated up the Tuna till the Captain arrived. Then Jerry and John, on acoustic guitar and stand-up bass, fed the deadheads a musical feast with a Ripple chaser.

Paul Krassner, *Realist* editor, Zen bastard, and heir apparent to the mantle of Lenny Bruce, did a tight twenty-five minutes of satire followed by the Shaman. This was a spectacular new age mellow-drama, developed at Camp Winnarainbow and orchestrated by Grateful Dead drummer Mickey Hart. The cast included a sick person, a "healer," a disease, several assorted angels (who dangled a hundred feet in the air attached to invisible rigging), and two dozen indigenous villagers who were drumming madly to aid the Shaman as he literally wrestled with the disease (played by Nirtan Lim). Also on stage were a boa constrictor, several live bunnies, and a couple of chickens. Needless to say, the good guys won.

Bob Weir did a short, sweet set with Brent Midland (God rest his soul) singing a spirited "Hey, Jude." Then along came Ken Kesey and the thunder machine, which is a marriage of musical metal and paint, created by the late Ron Boise and inhabited by Kesey's son, Zane. Ken told a tale he learned from his grandmother, and was backed up by a flock of Oregonian jazzsters who integrated beautifully with the thunder. Finally, came the latest combination of Jefferson Airplane parts called the KBC Band (as in Kantner, Balen, Cassidy).

Because it was my birthday I got to close the show. I did a two-tune medley of Classic Gravy. First came "Harpo's Ladder." On this silly sing-a-long the entire audience slips paper bags over their heads and performs the Funny Mantra, which is a razzberry vibration of lips on paper that turns everyone into a living kazoo. (You had to be there.)

We ended with my anthem, "Basic Human Needs." I was backed up brilliantly by the "Wavettes"—Suzi Barsotti, Jenny Muldaur, and my wife Jahanara, who seizes the microphone and says, "Wavy Gravy, we just couldn't let you orchestrate your entire birthday."

At which point they wheeled out this old-time bathtub painted gold and surrounded by fifty burning candles. The tub is full of chocolate pudding. The audience spontaneously breaks into a rousing rendition of "Happy Birthday" and it is evident that I am expected to blow out the candles. This will require formidable lung power as they are plumber's candles. Fifty plumber's candles—each one about an inch around and

placed three inches apart all the way around the tub. I begrudg-
ingly took a deep breath and bent to the task . . .

. . . when from out of the bottomless bowels of the pudding rose my (then fourteen-year-old) son Jordan wearing a
snorkel and goggles. My brain rolled straight out my ear and I
didn't even hear the flip.

I understand I attended a reception after the concert in the
Berkeley High School cafeteria. I'm told I was both witty and
charming, and helped to serve up countless cuts of a cake the
size of David Sobel, who owns the Bolinas Bakery where it was
born. I, of course, remember none of this because whatever
part of the cerebrum it is that remembers stuff was out bum-
ming around with the rest of my brain, out riding the rails of
heaven, forever toward the Fun.

Now it's your turn.

Begin with an interior "AAAHHHHH" and openings will
appear along the way. Fill them with serious fun, which is hard
work and fun sometimes.

HA!!!

My son Jordan rising from the pudding was first revealed
in a vision to long-time Hog farmer Loughrienne Nightgoose as
she was driving to the party from Big Mountain, Arizona. She
implored the creative process to come up with a real mind-
blower and the kachinas came and whispered in her ear.

AH HA!!!

Now for the actualization! Turning the flip into flop. Once
in Berkeley it was necessary for Goose to visit every supermar-
ket in the city in order to score enough of the powdered brown
stuff to fill an entire bathtub. Imagine the leers at the checkout
counter. All those tiny little boxes get folks talking.

"Hey Harry, look at that lady in aisle two. Heaven help her!"

"What's she on?"

"Pudding!"

No, dear reader, she is not on pudding. She is of the Loose Wig and is acting as a channel toward the train wreck of my mind. I owe her a big one. We all owe each other the sweet lick of liberation whenever possible. YUM. YUM!

Pull my thumb!

"PPPHHHHTTTTTTTTT!!!"

Pheeee Yeeew! Who cut one?

"Nobody cut one, silly. That's the sound of the funny mantra."

Well, that's the smelliest mantra I ever heard.

And the fart turns to fog and we slowly dissolve to . . .

Me, being a clown at the Children's Cancer Research Institute, which is a small unit within the Pacific Presbyterian Hospital in San Francisco. CCRI would be every kid's dream hangout except for the one-word ticket for admission: *leukemia*. The unit has toys and computer games, make-your-own sundaes, and an extremely dedicated staff which sometimes includes me as volunteer clown.

That's me now, putting clown-white makeup on little Billy. I often use makeup as a connection to children of all ages. I let them watch me put on my makeup and it helps to demystify the sometimes scary clown vibe. Billy was about eleven and needed no demystification. This kid was ready for anything. And so was his little sister, who said, "We could show the movie on Billy's head."

I looked down at my handiwork and sure enough, I had covered Billy's entire head with clown white. The chemo had long since claimed his hair so Billy was bald as a billiard ball, and his little sister was right! We could indeed show the movie on Billy's head. (We had Godzilla cued up to project on the wall of the day room instead.)

"Could we, Wavy Gravy? Could we please show Godzilla on my head?"

There was no way I could deny such a bizarre and heartfelt request.

"Okay Billy, you got it! But promise to tell me if your neck gets sore and we'll shoot the movie back up on the wall." I figured the kid wouldn't make it through the credits.

So there we all were, sitting around eating popcorn and watching Godzilla on Billy's head. Billy is positively glowing with delight and I must confess my mind had already entered the train wreck zone—just when I thought things couldn't possibly get any weirder . . . in walked a team of visiting Japanese doctors here to inspect the unit! Plop plop plop plop plop . . .

. . . and the sound of their brains softly splattering on the linoleum, to join mine in the pudding- and sandstone-swept vistas that lay in the light at the end of the tunnel of fun.

Woodstock, the First Hundred Years

"Let's see—weasel, world peace, won ton—here it is, Flanthe. Woodstock. It's a match! I feel the data oozing off the orb. Wavy Gravy was at Woodstock under his registered birth name, Hugh Romney. Let's see, born Hugh Nanton Romney, East Greenbush, New York, May 15, 1936.

"Zorb, dearest. Just skip the early life. Scroll down to the summer of twenty sixty nine—just before the hundredth anniversary," Flanthe suggested tactfully. "That would make Mr. Hugh 'Wavy Gravy' Romney one hundred and thirty-three years young. No spring chicken," said Zorb as he further consulted the primitive history orb. "I'm getting he participated in the BHT experiments of the twenty-first century. I'm getting— Yes! Flanthe, you are absolutely Geller on this. I get he made a hologram before discorporation—and it was a Lomax."

"Great work," said Flanthe excitedly. "Can you access?"

"We are accessed. It's going to be expensive. I'm billing it to your McDonald's," he replied, completing the necessary crystal work.

There was a bright buzz and the image took form and

solidified in the center of the pod. The two planetary anthropologists strapped in to watch. The buzz grew brighter and then the voice began to speak.

"This is Lomax Alan XXVL. Woodstock is one hundred— the Wavy Gravy Grams— Take five."

A very old and somewhat portly gentleman is seated on an equally ancient rocking chair on the front porch of the rambling lakeside simu-wood facility. A cheerfully hand-painted sign on the shingled wall reveals it to be Hog Heaven—Home for Aged Hippie Icons.

"What's that he's wearing?"

"They called it tie-duds. They certainly are colorful. Shhh! He's going to speak."

"My name is Wavy Gravy and I am one hundred and thirtysomething. I lost count when my wife died. She used to keep track of all that stuff. I always told folks that my chromosomes had amnesia but . . . I remember Woodstock. Yessirreebob, Woodstock wasn't held at Woodstock either. Bet you didn't know that, did you? They just wouldn't allow Woodstock at Woodstock. 'They' being the chamber of commerce and the terrified folks of that town. They took the promoters to court and made them move it somewhere else. All the way to White Lake and Bethel. They been kicking themselves in the butt ever since, but it sure didn't stop 'em from cashing in. Every shop in Woodstock sells Woodstock memorabilia, even though the festival was fifty miles away.

"A bunch of us Hog Farmers—did I say I was a Hog Farmer? That's the name of our Hippie commune. Folks called us that cuz we started out on a real hog farm with real hogs. We once ran one for president. First female black-and-white candidate for president. We sure broke a lot of ground with that one, but that's another story.

"Where was I? Oh, yeah. We had one painted school bus

full of Hog Farmers right there when the injunctions made 'em move. The Hog Farmers were helping clear land for campsites and fire trails.

"Most of the rest of us was livin' in Llano, New Mexico. This feller shows up at the summer solstice celebration we was having high in the mountains just outside Santa Fe. His name is Stan Goldstein and we knew him from when we had all the buses in New York City, and he shows up one afternoon and asks us to assist with this musical festival they're puttin' on in New York state that summer. We said we'll all be in New Mexico and he says, 'That's all right. We'll fly you there in an astrojet.' Well, we thought he was, as we used to say, one toke over the line. We didn't pay any attention to him until he popped up at the summer solstice with this fancy aluminum briefcase full of big-time data.

"Next thing you know, there's eighty-five of us New Mexico communards on an American Airlines astrojet flying to New York City. Eighty-five of us and fifteen Indians.

"Not just us Hog Farmers either. We had the cream of all the hippie communes in the state of New Mexico. I'll bet you didn't know that either. Well sir, when we come off that there aircraft there were all these reporter fellas there to greet us. I never saw so many TV cameras in all my born days.

"This one press guy tells me we have been hired to do the security. What we had agreed to do is clear trails, dig fire pits—I even ordered up a bear suit and a rubber shovel; should some hippie make a dumb fire I would pop up out of the bushes in a bear suit and blow his brain. Heh-heh-heh.

"Let's see—where was I? Oh yeah, this reporter says we are the security and I ask him if he feels secure and he says yes and I say, 'Well, it must be working' and he says, 'What are you going to use for crowd control?' and I said, 'Cream pies and seltzer bottles.' And they all wrote it down.

"We were then poured into some fancy tour buses and driven to White Lake, where we hitched up with our advance crew and the Merry Pranksters, who drove the great bus Furthur all the way from Oregon. We all had a big palaver with the promoters about this security business and discovered it was all true. Right then and there we created the Please Force. Tom Law and I were elected Please Chiefs and the password was 'I forgot.'

"We would be given first shot at dealing with any difficult or dangerous situation and if we couldn't cut it they would then send in the 'real' police. These were off-duty New York cops under the command of one Wes Pomeroy.

"When we were asked just how many security armbands we would need for our Please Force, Ken Babbs, the senior Prankster and ex-Marine Corps captain, upped and asked them right back, 'Just how many people are you expecting to attend this Aquarian Exposition, anyway?'—to which they replied, 'About two hundred thousand.'

" 'That'll be sufficient,' says Babbs—and you can see that really blew their minds. I think we settled on a couple hundred but we kept printing up more with a potato stamp someone made. Once things got under way we would go out into the crowd with a bunch of them in our pocket and whenever we saw somebody act in a responsible manner we'd give them a couple of armbands. They were bright red with a picture of a flying pig printed in white and her name was Pigasus. You probably guessed that. She was also represented in a giant papier mâché piñata put together by Paul Foster, who also painted the Flied Lice banner hanging over by the kitchen dome.

"The dome was built by our advance crew. The Hog Farm free kitchen was run by Lisa Law, Peter Whiterabbit, and my wife Jahanara. Back then we called her Bonnie Jean. They drove into New York City and scored a semi truck full of brown rice, oats, and other staples, along with plenty of fresh vegetables and countless kitchen supplies.

"Our feeding stations could service about ten thousand people a meal, which was only a dent in the actual attendance but probably covered everybody who was both broke and hungry. It was a never-ending chore to chop and cook for so many folks. By the time *Life* magazine took that color picture of the Hog Farm kitchen it was staffed by volunteers. We was mainly passed out in the bushes.

"That whole week leading up to Woodstock we ate like kings and queens, courtesy of Max Yasgur, the dairy farmer who rented out his field for the festival. Each morning he would send over these huge containers of fresh milk and yogurt.

"I bet you wonder if I ever met him. You bet I did. It happened at the family bulletin board. I had the carpenters saw a hole in it big enough to stick your head through and make a live announcement. I was announcing the baby race when ol' Max walked up with his family. So naturally they attended the event.

"We raced the kids in three heats: walkers, runners, and crawlers. It was a real family-type thing and our family was growing by the minute.

"As opening day grew closer and closer, police and farmers flushed hordes of hippies out of their fields and barns and sent 'em to work for us if they wanted to earn a ticket. We would sign them up to one of the various crews. We had crews for the kitchen or the fire pits or the carpenter collective. We even had crews to man the information booths spread all over the site. All workers received tickets and free food.

"Just before opening day we took all these leftover telephone poles and built us an enormous bonfire. Those poles just cried out for the world's largest marshmallow. For some reason it was impossible to create a marshmallow from scratch. We were forced to drive around and buy up all the marshmallows in a five-mile radius. Then we mushed them together and used a pitchfork to stick them in the fire. By then we numbered close to five hundred souls and this was some of the sticky goo that glued us together.

"When the day of the show finally arrived, somehow the ticket turnstiles were not quite set up yet and thousands of people began streaming out onto the infield.

"Suddenly, one of the box-office guys runs up to me and Tom Law. We have been watching the whole thing go down. He says we should start clearing out the people cuz they are almost ready to start takin' tickets.

"Well sir, there were about twenty thousand warm bodies just sitting there in that cow pasture waiting for the show to start. Tom and me, we sort of looked at each other and simultaneously said, 'Do you want a good movie or a bad movie!' We heard they had just sold the movie rights to Warner Brothers for a tidy six-figure sum. Well, this guy goes running off and calls Mel Lawrence and Michael Lang on the walkie-talkie. Michael is the curly-haired whiz kid who thought this whole thing up in the first place and Mel was his logistics advisor. They huddled up for a minute or two and sure enough decided to make the whole thing a free festival! When the word got out about that, it gridlocked the New York State Thruway.

"The reason I got to do all those stage announcements was because of my relationship with Chip Monk. Chip built the stage at Woodstock. We went all the way back to when I was a hip tongue dancer doing stand-up at the Village Gate, where he practically invented concert lighting. Chip has a voice on a P.A. like a melted Hershey bar being poured in your ear.

* * *

" 'If you have taken the green acid you have just been poisoned!'

"I am paraphrasing here. It may have been brown acid but whatever color it was, each color had a lot of variations. Twenty shades of green in a crowd of a half million was not that unusual.

"Well, sir, ol' Chip makes that announcement and we got a rush hour at the freakout tent.

"That's what we called our unit of hog farmers engaged in talking down concertgoers from an excess of psychotropics, or "bum trips," as we used to call 'em in the old days. We were temporarily overwhelmed with a pulsating wave of alleged trippers. That's when I ran up that long ramp to the big stage and Chip let me make the announcement that all the green acid isn't poisoned and if they was in doubt they should give the guy who sold it to 'em half a tab and see what he does.

"I was so anxious to get the word out, it didn't really hit me that I was talking to so many people—so what I said had a soothing effect on the collective head. All this has been analyzed to tears by historians and is recorded on the original celluloid version along with my immortal, 'Good morning, what we have in mind is breakfast in bed for four hundred thousand.'

"Or was it five hundred thousand? Ever since Woodstock, officials have been asking me to estimate how many people have showed at any given event as if I possess these supernormal estimating sensors. I tell 'em to just count their legs and divide by two.

"I think the Hugh Romney construct at Woodstock World is very realistic, right down to the wart on my left cheek. I also appreciate their reenactment of our distribution of granola in Dixie cups to the multitudes in their muddy sleeping bags. The original of that act was the first recorded exposure of granola to hippies.

"Their response—'What is this shit? It looks like gravel.'—was deleted for the theme-park audios. I couldn't care less about that. What really sticks in my craw is the importation of French mud for the audience simulations. I hated that and the adverts: 'Lay in the mud and talk to Jimi.'

"The best thing about Woodstock World is that they built it in Woodstock and left the Bethel–White Lake area pristine for spiritual pilgrims.

"It is important to remember on this hundredth anniversary that the true meaning of Woodstock was spiritual. My line about how 'there is a little bit of heaven in every disaster area' was a realized truth.

"When Janis Joplin said, 'If you have any food left, share it with your brother and sister. That's the person on your right and the person on your left,' it was a realized truth. When people reacted to that sacred advice they got a deep print on the goodness of sharing. It just covered that crowd like a carpet of god. You just had to surrender your 'you' to that feeling. I gave up my own personal self early on. Then I experienced an inrush of energy that just danced me through my daily duties as they unfolded moment by moment.

"Whenever I thought it was just me doin' that stuff, I'd fall on my ass in the mud.

"Howdy Doody had more free will than I did on those three days in August of 1969. Three days of peace and love."

Lomax XXVI: "Was it really that peaceful? And why do you suppose that was?"

Gravy: "Well, sir, I think it was all that attention, when we got declared an official disaster area with a rock-and-roll soundtrack. That and the fact that we all knew the whole world was watching. We knew that we was living history. It was a chance to show the world how it could be if we were running the show.

"I remember early on, these two cowboys wanted to get into a fist fight near the front of the stage and five hundred thousand people yelled 'Peace,' and it cascaded over these cowboys and scared the living shit out of them. Once they stopped shaking in their boots they shook hands and the crowd roared. Talk about setting a tone. We all rose up to our highest common denominator and reflected it nationwide through the popular press. Peace was possible. And not just your run-of-the-mill peace with people not hurting each other, but a just peace full of stuff like sharing and caring.

"At first I thought we would seize control of the country and turn the whole death thing around. I thought we'd be the stockbrokers and senators and soothsayers of change. When that didn't happen right away I became a little disillusioned. Then I saw the spirit of Woodstock start to surface in our children and our children's children. I see it now in their quest for a just and lasting peace on earth and space. One hundred, no, a thousand years could pass away from those fateful August afternoons, and yet those holy vibes shall sail eternal through the stars.

"Yes sir. What I have in mind today is breakfast in bed for about four billion."

Snap crackle pop pop sizzle.

"Zorb, the orb is smoking—disengage! disengage!" cried Flanthe.

Zorb quickly extracted the red-hot access crystal from the grid, throwing the pod in darkness till the auxiliaries kicked in.

"Wow, that old geezer could really spew the quail. His bio says he did over fifty years in planetary politics and it shows. The quail was nearly knee deep when your McDonald's expired," said Flanthe.

"I got everything I need for my next infusion in 'Akeshik

Archeology,' replied Zorb, as he calmly poured out the ritual mixture of fruit, nuts, and grain.

"Happy Woodstock, Zorb," said Flanthe as they ceremoniously snorted the granola.

The Hog Farm Today

It almost didn't happen, this expanded family commune of mine. If Ken Babbs hadn't highjacked the good bus Furthur and hightailed it south to hook up with Ken Kesey in Mexico, effectively stranding most of the Merry Pranksters in Hollywood, there might never have been a Hog Farm.

We were posing for the cover of *Life* magazine when Babbs excused himself for a piss. My wife and I were also at that historic shoot. We observed the look of abject horror on the faces of our cohorts as the full impact of those fading taillights hammered home. *Never trust a Prankster.*

We had no recourse but to invite our abandoned brothers and sisters to spend the night at our tiny little cabin in the country. It seems like it was almost yesterday that our landlord instantly evicted us when he discovered we had over twenty house guests ensconced all over our one-bedroom spread.

It took almost two hours for the Universe to conjure up our deliverance in the person of our neighbor, one Bud Pelsu, who came by in his battered pickup truck to suggest we move up to that place on the mountain. It seems old Saul had just had a stroke and they needed somebody to slop them hogs.

It took three years for us to load up that mountain and hit

the road in a convoy of buses packed full of humans and one baby hog who would one day run for president.

We spent close to ten tight years rambling the highways and biways of the Planet Earth before we ran out of gas. Like the pilgrims of Plymouth we landed in the New World of Berkeley, California, in quest of shelter and some kind of right livelihood.

Magic and providence had fueled our mobile hallucination for nearly a decade. Now it was time for us to earn our money the old-fashioned way and actually get a job. And so it was that we hippies moved to Babylon. This was the telephone answering service we all helped to found. Farming phones instead of pigs. "Hi, can I help you. . . . Hi, can I help you Hi, can I help you. . . . Please hold!!!"

It is now the summer of '91 and Babylon the great has fallen. The person you have just reached is not a working person . . . please hang yourself up. We have sold our phone business and have become considerably diversified. We Hogs have somehow parlayed our sprawling southside haven into the hippie Hyannisport we inhabit in the north of Berkeley today. We are also in the process of purchasing the Black Oak Ranch, a six-hundred-acre piece of paradise about three-and-a-half-hours north of San Francisco, just past the sleepy town of Laytonville.

This is our Hog Heaven on earth. Here we find the summertime home of Camp Winnarainbow; the teepee and awning business called Intents; Martin's Modules, a large organic garden; a hundred and fifty sheep; Stan's Jam; Nobody's Business; Bioengineering Associates; and Evan Engber's business, which gets government grants to heal the earth. Our Black Oak Ranch camp facility has also rented to the Seva Foundation for their summer board meeting, and to the Tennessee Farm for its

1991 reunion. Let us tastefully arrange your wedding, retreat, or bar mitzvah.

The ranch in Laytonville is the launching pad for all our dreams and aspirations. Someday soon, I suspect, we will fold up our Berkeley operation and rest all our weary eggs in this one final basket. On Labor Day 1990, we hosted the Hog Farm twenty-five-year reunion and had a record number of attendees—almost four hundred.

How do we do it? How have we stayed together for so long while the great communes of the sixties collapsed by the wayside? The answers are the same for my marriage to Jahanara. Chalk it up to love, slack, and a good sense of humor. No matter what the media said about us, we never bought into our own myth. We always solve our problems in a circle. We are each a cog in the collective hog, although the tracks of the elders are honored and respected.

Consensus was almost our downfall. We now are a consensus-minus-one operation. The Hog Farm can have one true fanatic and still get things done. Many of the early communes were too gung-ho for their own good. Everything was sacrificed to the group. Not so in our scene. People put into the common pot whatever feels right to them. We have fair shares and rent but whatever is put in beyond this is an individual decision. It is possible to be a millionaire and be a Hog Farmer if you pay your fair share. Your millions are your business.

But before you can become a land partner all the other land partners have a year to suss you out. It is very much like a marriage, and a mass marriage at that. You can wheedle your way into the scene with tenacity, good vibes, and rent. The whole hog loves a hard worker and we are easily hoodwinked by folks who show up and wash a tubful of dishes and volunteer for all the shit jobs. They usually do this until they are somewhat ingratiated into the scene and then they hang around until they are asked to leave.

We have seen many incarnations of this particular type and have learned to beware geeks bearing gifts. They generally come with their stuff and they generally don't leave without it. I tend to be like water over rock and am real forgiving. Every breath is another chance for a person to change his or her behavior for the better. I try to see the best in everyone. Thank god my nonbiological brothers and sisters are not so naive.

I have absolute faith in the "group brain" and after twenty-five years I have seen us learn from our mistakes and not take our successes for granted. I wish I could say the same for myself personally. Ah well, love and learn. I recently scanned a copy of *Intentional Communities* at a local bookstore and was proud to see us modestly listed. However, it was impossible to tell from the listing just how one went about joining the Hog Farm.

This was ever thus. Even in the ancient times when we lived on the buses it was a great mystery. We would wake up one morning and some stranger would be sleeping in the wheel well or the driver's seat. Through a series of circumstances that were always different, they either stayed awhile or disappeared before our very eyes. We still have a three-day rule for visitors but they must be sponsored by a living hog farmer in order to qualify.

Back to *Intentional Communities.* I was really impressed by just how many listings there were. It helps bear out my theory that there are many more communes existing today than in the sixties. It makes good ecological and financial sense to live with a group of people today.

I myself could toil several lifetimes and never own my own six-hundred-acre spread with two separate lakes (one with a three-hundred-fifty-foot water slide), not to mention the garage and the workshop and the teepee factory and sheep barn and clinic and tractor and backhoe and dump truck and buses and trailers and houses and kids' camp and graveyard. . . .

Yet our true wealth is each other and the bonds that we have forged in our first quarter-century. We are currently carpenters and contractors and sun dancers and clowns. We are doctors and midwives and shopkeepers and cooks. We are reporters and artists and attendants and musicians and children and wizards and designers of dreams. We seem to be simultaneously living our dream and dreaming our life. We are working for peace on a planet that is healthy and whole. We are working for justice for indigenous people and a good life for our kids. We are playing and praying for our lives.

If we can do it, so can you. Just get your gang together and pool what is comfortable. It helps to live together and eat at least one common meal a day. Try to get everyone to take turns cooking. The first lessons revolve around the stomach.

Feed yourself and your family, feed the world. The most sacred books on the Hog Farm are the *I Ching* and *Joy of Cooking*. That cookbook begins with a quote from Goethe's *Faust*. If you take the trouble to look it up it may prove useful. After all, you're the boss here, dear reader. We are just words on a page that only you can turn. Our future lies in your fingers, eyes, and heart. So turn, turn, turn.

Peanuts in My Hamburger

She put peanuts in my hamburger and she glowed just like a goddess at the grill. I didn't see her do it and wondered why she grinned as I bit into the bun, tore through both tomato and lettuce, almost missing the whisper of mayo as I began to encounter the beef. It was not until my second mastication that the peanuts kicked in.

Peanuts! This woman actually placed a handful of peanuts in the center of my beef patty. Then she cooked it to perfection and served it up with a frosty mug of pre-Prankster cherry Kool-Aid. She seemed all but oblivious of her beauty. A Maria Schell movie-star face, framed by her North Country honey-blond hair, which was backlit by the Wurlitzer blasting Furry Lewis in the night.

Her name was Bonnie Jean Beecher, a.k.a. Country Pie, and she ran the joint. The joint was the Fred C. Dobbs and it was the hippest of the hip new restaurants adorning Sunset Boulevard at the time. It had good food, a killer jukebox, and its far-out clientele included Marlon Brando and the Byrds.

She waved her spatula like a scepter as the peanuts hit my tastebuds and exploded all the flashbulbs in the cameras of my mind. I knew at that moment I had found my true person and lifetime companion. I sat gawking in utter disbelief as I studied this interior photo as it floated in and out of focus.

I just couldn't believe this was happening to me. I was still reeling from a failed marriage to a beautiful woman, and my mind was still gibbering Silly Putty from the psychedelically inspired inner knowledge that there was something to this God shit after all.

I was a hip, cool, emotional basket case and was certifiably terrified of all beautiful women. Bonnie Jean Beecher was a beautiful and budding young television actress who had just buried her lover after he totaled her truckful of tiles bound for the counters of the Fred C. Dobbs.

We were both severely shattered and somehow, through the grace of God, we got to be each other's glue. Within two years we would be husband and wife. Our knot was officially tied in a quaint New England chapel nestled in delightful downtown Las Vegas.

Naturally, we honey-mooned at Disneyland.

A high point of the honeymoon was the aborted trip we took through the looking glass on the Alice in Wonderland ride. We were comfortably snuggling in our seats as our car entered the tunnel of make-believe. I vaguely remember the disembodied smile of the Cheshire cat dispelling the darkness until we were jolted to an abrupt stop.

Suddenly, the place was ablaze with bright lights, revealing a cadre of white-coated technicians scampering aimlessly about, shouting, "Alice is down! Alice is down!"

In our more than twenty-five-year adventure of wedded bumps and bliss, when the bottom would fall out of our dreams and desires, we had only to utter "Alice is down" to get a little humor and perspective.

In hindsight, married life is a pitful of pitfalls designed by some devious deity for our conscious evolution. Along with those pitfalls comes an occasional pasture of plenty that is thrown in at random to humanize the race. I realized right away that a wife was a whole lot more than an extension of her husband, which was what my early Eisenhower existence had incorrectly indicated. It took me about five years to dechauvinize.

Gibran's sweet advice on marriage helped me bridge the pitfalls with paradox and find the spaces in our togetherness, but it was A. E. Orage who saved our marriage with his essay on love.

It happens occasionally in the realm of human experience that a match occurs between the heart and the intellect, and we just *get it*. My marriage was going to hell in a handbasket—a souped-up solar-powered handbasket at that. I was open and ready to receive the living truth of A. E.'s essay on conscious perfect love.

Conscious perfect love is when you love someone so completely that you wish only for your beloved's self-realization. That they are given the space and the wherewithal to discover who they are without any thought of reciprocation or reward for one's self. Orage goes on to say that this quality is often displayed by human beings to, say, a race horse, but seldom to a fellow human.

This was just the kind of challenge I needed to break on through to the other side. You see, I tend to thrive on the impossible and I really loved my wife. I captured the entire situation in a song I wrote that helped free us both for future growth and happiness.

> *Take whatever you need to be you, Bonnie Jean*
> *Take whatever you need to be you.*
> *Take what you need*
> *don't care i bleed*

use my soul for the bottom of your shoe.
Conscious perfect love is for you, precious frog,
Conscious perfect love is for you.

Grab you hold tightly
and let you go lightly.
It sure took us time to crack through!
You can stomp on my grave
and I'll stand up and wave
take whatever you need to be you.

For the last twenty years, in faithfully following this path of conscious perfect love, I have watched my wife evolve from a talented television actress who ran away with a busful of hippie Hog Farmers bound for heaven knows where by way of California and Katmandu. I saw her embrace Sufism and take on the spiritual teacher who re-named her Jahanara. Today, Jahanara is chairperson of the Seva Foundation and co-director of Camp Winnarainbow. She is also my wife, friend, and fellow pilgrim on the path. We live in separate rooms in the Hog Farm complex in Berkeley, and like young lovers we hop from room to room.

Jah and I are living testament to the possibility of the impossible as we continue to pursue our separate but parallel lives in conscious perfect love. Occasionally, Alice drops down to visit, and we are never, never bored.

Pick a Nose

I was hunkered down next to my Christmas-tree-light-festooned shopping cart and listening to Laurie Anderson bending the sound barrier at New York's Cathedral of St. John the Divine when the stage manager scampered over and caught my attention.

"What is it this time?" I hollered in his ear.

"David Crosby is very unhappy backstage and it looks like he may walk," he said.

I did my best version of bounding over the stage-right monitors and other minor obstructions that divided backstage from the rest of the world. David and Graham weren't due on for ages. We still had Sweet Honey in the Rock, Mickey Hart, Michael Hinton, and Olitunji to go plus Paul Simon, Carly Simon, and the Tibetan Gyoto Monks (not together, but all unannounced on the program). Also set to appear to read passages from literature concerning the plight of the homeless were an ensemble of actors—Willem Dafoe, Margot Kidder, and Susan Sarandon. Allen Ginsberg would read his new epic poem "The White Shroud."

When I got backstage everybody was just kinda standing around in the hallway. There really isn't very much backstage to a gothic cathedral. It took me a couple of minutes to find the Crosby and Nash Crypt. I had to admit it was a tad dank and gloomy inside. I stood next to this intricately carved sarcophagus and surveyed the situation. Something had David Crosby fried. A tiny black cloud hovered just over his head.

I was clad in the crumbling remains of my original Prankster can't-bust-me jumpsuit with the "kick me"–style sign stuck on my back that said "Homeless but Horny." In an attempt to appear serious I removed my giant clown nose. I parked it on the first sensible protrusion I could find. This turned out to be the white marble nose of the bishop buried below us, whose likeness was carved on the lid of the sarcophagus. That simple, uncalculated act may have saved the show.

All I know is David's cloud instantly parted and he commenced to roar a rainbow of laughter at the sight of my clown nose perfectly perched on that sacred marble schnozzola. I gave the Cos a big hug and headed back to bring on Sweet Honey. I never found out what the fuss was all about but maybe we were saved by a nose.

I named my nose Heaven and it instantly became my most prized possession . . . which I lost the following evening gambling with Ram Dass.

Dissolve to the following evening.

We are in Tuxedo, New York, attending the mid-year board meeting of the Seva Foundation. We are deep into our tremendously busy agenda—discussing Seva's deepening role in the Nepal Blindness program, and our collaboration with Aravind Eye Hospital in India, which does more free eye surgery than any other clinic in the world—when we get wind of our possible appearance on "Entertainment Tonight." A TV is quickly lined up for that possibility.

Meanwhile we keep on meeting. Meet, meet, meet. At seven o'clock the TV was illuminated (with the sound off) in case they aired our segment. I, for one, was watching Mary

Hart with one eye and the Seva agenda with the other. My eyes were as crossed as my fingers. I felt it would be a big-time boon if millions of Americans heard what transpired the previous evening at the Cathedral of St. John the Divine.

After about ten minutes of mindless tabloid titillation the Seva board gave in to curiosity overload, and turned up the sound. We were all totally exhausted, having spent the previous day and night working on the homeless benefit in one capacity or other. Our prospects were looking bleak as they cut to the final commercial. I looked limply into Ram Dass' likewise limpid orbs. "It's not happening," he ventured.

"Wanna bet?" sez I.

And so it was I bet my sacred Heaven nose against his likewise sacred mallah beads. The mallah, or Hindu rosary, was of Belgian crystal with a sterling guru-bead. The nose, although a modest ball of crimson foam rubber, had burst the mighty Cos's funk.

It was a good bet, well made, yet hardly sealed when the ad for Endust ended and the tube was seized by the Seva celebration for the homeless.

First there were shots of our pre-concert reception and an interview with Robin Williams. He spoke eloquently for the cause. In the background you could faintly hear Dr. John's piano and Maria Muldaur. Then they zoomed inside the cathedral for a quick lick of Laurie Anderson and a snip of the Crosby, Simon (Carly), and Nash sound check done earlier that afternoon.

In a flash the spot was finished. Over, Done. *Big deal.* We got about three minutes on a program that some critics maintain was created for a public that doesn't possess the attention span to make it through *People* magazine. I, however, thought we scored access to a whole new segment of the population who would be stirred by the piece to do something to help the homeless.

I certainly know I scored this boss set of beads from the Dass man. These beads were the mama of all mallahs. I stayed up half the night trying to count my way into clown bliss, but this time it seemed somewhat hollow. I started feeling sorry for Ram Dass, and couldn't sleep. Although he was a beautiful loser, I decided I shouldn't have been so quick to grab his beads and boogie. To appease my gnawing guilt I stood before the Baba that morning at breakfast. In one clenched fist I held the mallah beads, in the other fist was the Heaven nose. It was time for him to choose . . . again.

He chose the Heaven nose and I absconded with the beads. It was a clean take this time. Later that morning I presented him with a rainbow fright-wig and a full set of Krylon clown paint to complement his newly acquired clown nose. (Just in case the cosmos has a Baba Bozo somewhere up its sacred sleeve.)

Apex with Seva

The absolute apex of my life as a benefit concert organizer occurred on the vernal equinox (June 21), 1984, at an event at the Kingswood Amphitheater just outside of Toronto, featuring The Band and the Grateful Dead.

I came on stage first and introduced the Band with *Enthusiasm,* which is a hexigram from the *I Ching* or the *Chinese Book of Changes.* I told of how the hexigram describes music as being a bridge between the seen and the unseen. The hexigram goes on to invite all our ancestors to be present at the concert. As I read, I can feel an incredible wave of energy sweep over the entire audience, and I am lifted to rock-and-roll-benefit heaven. If it was any better I couldn't stand it. There were two of my favorite musical cabals playing to a full house and the proceeds were going to aid the good work of Seva, my favorite charity. How sweet it was!

Seva is derived from a Sanskrit word for service. Its board of directors is composed mainly of doctors and health-care workers who helped to spearhead the world-wide eradication of smallpox, while in the service of the World Health Organization (WHO). The Seva Foundation was created in an attempt to reflect that same dedication and to use the appropriate technology to help reduce human suffering, but to operate without the ponderous bureaucracy of WHO.

Ram Dass is on the board of Seva. So is Danny Rifkin, the

long-time manager of the Grateful Dead. And me, too, I've been with Seva since it was founded over thirteen years ago, as has my wife Jahanara, who served as our 1990–91 chairperson. I am the chief FUNd raiser on the Seva board. That's capital F-U-N, small d; and the Third Eyeball sure generated plenty of both—funds and fun for our projects in Nepal and India.

As the title might imply, Seva is involved in the prevention and cure of unnecessary blindness. It seems that 80 percent of the blindness in the world is preventable and 80 percent of that is reversible. The price of a cataract operation at a mobile eye camp in Nepal was about the same price as a ticket to our benefit concert in Canada. The eye operation takes about ten minutes. The bandages are removed in seven days.

The concert that day took about four hours. What a rush it was to participate, even indirectly, in both amazing activities. The audience that afternoon represented over seventeen thousand saved eyeballs. Extra funds came from people sitting in the circle of gold. Those people kicked in extra bucks to be up close, and also got to attend a reception we held in the Japanese Tea House just after the concert. It is always an excellent idea to have a reception before or after any event. In certain situations the money I've collected from those receptions has made up almost half my gross, and it's a way to thank all the people who worked to put on the show.

The Japanese Tea House is part of the theme park that is connected to the Kingswood Amphitheater. Featured there is a thrill ride called "Hell in a Bucket," named after a song by Bobby Weir of the Dead. Weir came to the reception and stayed till they kicked us out. So did Mickey Hart. Band members Rick Danko and Levon Helm showed up and sat in with Sylvia Fricker and her swell country band, The Great Speckled

Bird. Fans present at the reception were real respectful and gave the artists plenty of space to relax.

True, there were some autographs gleaned to grace our "killer" poster. Posters are very important. I always try to create an eye-catching advertisement for events; not only does it help get the word out, but the sale of posters as well as T-shirts adds revenue to a cause. Our T-shirts, however, were held up in Customs and didn't arrive until midway through the Dead's set. Bummer!

Why did I go all the way to a foreign country for the venue, you might ask? Well, Seva is also represented in Canada by the Seva Service Society and money raised there is matched and sometimes doubled by the Canadian International Development Agency. "Double Our Money" was a major incentive in our decision to go over the border.

Many years before, the Grateful Dead were turned inside out by Canadian customs, who were suspicious of a bottle of vitamins belonging to one of the band members. Mickey Hart was so traumatized that time, he made me promise to comfort him if the agents ever again explored his orifices with a flashlight. Such is the lot of the poor producer, and should be accepted graciously and without complaint. This time around, we had a pro expedite the crossing. If only our T-shirts had been so lucky. Now we know to always allow plenty of extra time for international shipping.

I also had to raise an additional ten thousand dollars to pay for the satellite uplink for National Public Radio. I thought it would be extra terrific if we could broadcast our whole show throughout the United States on NPR. The Grateful Dead do this every New Year's Eve, and occasionally for something special like this show.

That 10K was very hard for me to come by. I have a certain skill at getting artists to contribute their talent to a good cause. Seva is an easy sell. We are the best bang for the buck in all of benefitland. Our projects are well run and most of the money goes just where the donors intended it. There is a neat clean line of trust from the heart to the wallet to the field. Seva's overhead is also quite respectable. For many years it came only from earmarked funds. I have a real flair for passing a hat in a crowd, but it is sheer hell for me to phone up big corporations and convince wealthy executives to make a thousand-dollar donation to *What? A radio show?* It was way easier for me to get the bands to commit.

The Dead have been helping us out since our inception. The first Seva benefit was held at the Oakland Auditorium. Most of the attendees weren't aware it was a benefit until halfway through the show. Bill Graham was just as surprised as they were. After he adjusted to this unforeseen reality he walked over to where I was standing in the wings and handed me an enormous personal check to Seva. I said, "Bill, why are you doing this?"

"Because you did not hit on me, my friend."

Bill Graham has always been there with his company, ready to produce for any good cause that has attracted talent big enough to sell the number of tickets needed for the event to be successful.

Donations to Seva from Francis Carr of Manor Downs and Ahmet Ertegun of Atlantic Records moved the radio uplink closer. David Geffen bit my head off, so I grew a new head and somehow raised the remaining money.

Ken Kesey and Paul Krassner were our radio hosts, and the whole darn thing was beamed up to a satellite in space, which bounced it back to Lawrence, Kansas, where my friend Steve DiNafrieo spun it out to subscribing PBS stations nationwide. What a great boon it was for Seva to get its message out to so large and diverse an audience.

It was a great joy for me to introduce The Band in Canada. Even without Robbie Robertson they were still the reigning royalty of Canadian rock-and-roll. I have loved these guys forever and have become good friends with every one of them.

When the show was first a go, a press conference was held with Weir and Garcia, along with some of the Band. Weir had adopted Seva as his favorite charity some years before. It was kinda like a marriage for both parties. Many artists pick one or two causes that they can relate to for their prime focus of doing good in the world. After all, we only have so much juice to go around and there are so many worthy endeavors.

These days I only put shows together for Seva. I will act as advisor or master of ceremonies for all types of wonderful stuff, but I only ask artists to perform for Seva. I write this in the hope that it will spare me some of the letters and phone calls I deal with every day from good people who want me to produce their show or at least help them line up the Grateful Dead. Please spare me. Only the Dead can get the Dead to do anything, and even this is not a given.

Here are some tips for producing your own benefit:

Try to get a direct line to the artist. Managers and agents are often engaged by the artists as a buffer between them and the countless requests they get to do benefits. Don't be discouraged if they don't return your calls. I remember being particularly bummed when some manager didn't call me back. Bill Graham popped it in perspective: "You got to remember, Wavy, ten percent of nothin' is nothin'." So don't get paranoid, just keep chippin' away at it. All they can do is say no. And it only takes a couple of yeses to build your show.

Make sure that all your yeses can attract an audience. It may come as a shock to hear that *most benefits lose money*. This can be avoided be checking to see if your acts are a draw before you accept their generous offer to perform. Many groups are desperate for any kind of exposure and sometimes this is a wonderful opportunity for everyone concerned. If your organization can sell a lot of tickets to its own membership, you can focus on the aesthetic rather than the commercial aspects of the show.

If your show does well, you have the potential to make it an annual event. These become easier to sell tickets to with each successful year. If your show is well produced, word gets around.

Always procure a good sound system and a skilled technician to run it. You can skimp a little on other production values, like venue and lighting, but if the show sounds bad everybody loses—the audience, the artist, and you. If you are a bona fide nonprofit charity, many sound companies will give you a discount.

Never put money down on a date before you line up your talent. Most auditoriums will hold several dates for a limited time. You'll be surprised how the choice of more than one date makes the mix-and-match of putting a show together that much easier. Once you have all the talent in tow, allow at least six to eight weeks to promote your show.

I spent nearly a month in Canada working on the Third Eyeball. Because of the scope of the event, we hired Richard Flohill part-time. Flohill is by far Toronto's finest publicist, and boy did he ever get the word out. Everything was timed to perfection.

If your event is a genuine benefit you are entitled to free listings in the newspapers, and on radio and television stations. It is a must to send your press releases to the public service director or datebook listings person within their necessary lead time. Then—and this is very important—you must call back and make sure your release has been received, and (if possible) that it is being implemented. The media is constantly assailed with entertainment notices, many of which slip through the cracks. It is often a given to have a certain amount of pay advertising in the popular press. Try to find the best timetable for your ads, and see if there is any possibility of a feature article prior to the event.

It is a good idea to check with the artists and their management for their availability to do a phone or in-person interview before the performance. We really lucked out in Canada because our artists were so committed to the success of the concert, we were able to pull off the press conference. This was slapped together exquisitely by Dick Flohill and was held at Toronto's Bamboo Club during an afternoon when the club was inactive. Bob and Jerry flew in from Buffalo where they happened to be performing that weekend. Such windows of opportunity are rare and must be pounced upon with great vigor. Danny Rifkin was key in all Dead-related doings, and was invaluable to me in dealing with ticket sales and the heavies at Kingswood.

It is a very warm feeling to sell out your show in advance and not have to rely on the crap-shoot of a walk-up attendance. We worked very hard for our sellout. The folks at Seva Canada had me doing an interview every four hours during the final two weeks before the show. The best advertising in the world *is* word of mouth. Its benefits, however, don't generally kick in until you have achieved a certain quantum mass, and that only comes about after a lot of work, from the organization of an opening press conference to each flyer handed out on the street. The rule of thumb is ten flyers equal one attendee.

Don't feel you have to start out with a mega-event like the Third Eyeball. Start small and do it in your own community. Beware of fast talkers who want to get you Bob Dylan and the Rolling Stones on world satellite TV. Don't feel it's the end of the world if you don't make money every time.

My first big Seva event was at Carnegie Hall in New York City. "Sing Out for Sight" featured lots of old folkies: Odetta, Tom Paxton, Bob Gibson, Peter Yarrow, Happy Traum, Peter Rowan, the Josh White Singers. We had an extremely successful press conference at the United Nations, a fabulous performance, and lost about three thousand dollars at the box office.

Why did I lose money on such a great show? Well, since you asked, Carnegie Hall is not cheap and I booked the show on the eve of Yom Kippur, when many of my potential audience were off knoshing at their parents'. I have since done several successful incarnations of the "Sing out for Sight" format. To assure success, in addition to the usual assemblage of folk acts I get a couple of red-hot rockers to unplug and play acoustic. We've had Jerry and Bobby, Jorma Kaukonen, Rick Danko, Crosby, Stills, and Nash, Paul Simon, Dr. John, Bonnie Raitt, and Stevie Ray Vaughn, to name a few. We sold out nearly every show.

So that's it. To review, here are the two secrets of success:

1. Never count your money till it's spent.
2. Never, ever book a show on Yom Kippur.

Now you're in the benefit business.

My Fan

It had been one of those strange kinda days. I had already nearly run into a couple of yaks in the fog on the San Diego freeway.

I roared my Packard Caribbean convertible into the nearest Shell station at full babble: *"There are yaks on the freeway!"* The attendant assured me that there were indeed yaks on the freeway, and they were being taken care of as we spoke. It seems that they broke out of their holding pen at the San Diego Zoo and disappeared in the morning fog. I was so relieved I nearly kissed the guy.

Instead, I put my pedal to the metal and continued climbing up into Santa Barbara, where I had a gig that night at a café in the hills. I am Hugh Romney—former teen-age beatnik turned tongue dancer and hip comic—on a mini-tour of the country to promote my brand new album, "Hugh Romney: Third Stream Humor."

When I pulled up, the joint was packed. I hit the can to throw a couple handfuls of cold water on my face and then I hit the stage. The house manager gave me a great introduction and the audience enthusiastically applauded. I could tell already, this was an artist's dream. I cocked back my head to let 'er rip when this voice comes booming from the back of the house: "I AM THE ALBATROSS."

I could only squint into the spotlights as he said once again, "I AM THE ALBATROSS."

This time I lashed back, "And I'm John James Audubon," and I pretend to sketch him on an invisible tablet with my equally invisible crayon. "Please stand very still."

I was proud of myself for coming up with such a quick retort for the heckler. In fact, most of the audience thought it was part of my act. The more I denied it, the more they were certain I was putting them on.

I slipped into some well-memorized material and went on automatic while I scanned this albatross dude for sanity. He appeared to be a twenty-five-year-old white Anglo-Saxon male with sandy brown hair. He had these big black pupils. I mean, his eyes were without irises and he was looking at me big-time.

I finished the bit and took a quick time-out. I then proceeded to drag the house manager into the tiny kitchen and asked him to send for some kind of psychiatric assistance. It took nearly half an hour for the men in the actual white coats to arrive and net this guy. By the time they showed up, he had emptied the house with his ornithological antics and low-flying drool. As this poor deranged soul was being forcibly lifted out the door in a straitjacket, he looked me straight in the eye and screamed, "But I'm your Fan!"

The intensity of his outcry made me pause on the cusp of a promising career and ask myself if I really wanted to pursue this showbiz lifestyle. I imagined myself trapped with a whole roomful of such individuals—and so did the house manager as he pondered the plausibility of holding me over for another night. We both decided this was an isolated incident and pressed on with our lives.

I finished the tour at the Village Gate in New York City. I think I was opening for John Coltrane or Thelonius Monk. Afterward, I bumped into Bobby Dylan on Macdougal Street, which was not all that uncommon before he was washed by the waters of fame and fortune. We got into a deep rap about the future of the Gaslight Cafe. I had a small room up above the club, which I sometimes shared with Dylan. He wrote "Hard Rain" there on my rusty old Remington.

Suddenly, Dylan tugs me into this darkened doorway. He is peering furtively across the street at this guy walking by.

"Let's just wait here for a minute, man. Do you see that guy over there? Do you know who that guy is?"

When I told him I didn't, he told me he didn't either but would I mind hanging out till the object of his attention went around the corner. I had no problem with that. Dylan was definitely a great choice for someone I'd enjoy lurking in a doorway with in 1962. He was extremely funny then and had an opinion about everything. That he would choose to express these opinions in a doorway to avoid an imaginary encounter with an anonymous stranger I found a tad paranoid. At that time, few people were familiar with Dylan and those who knew him were mostly folk-heads, a gentle and respectful bunch. Perhaps he had perceived his rock-and-roll future in those early furtive glances.

Ten years would pass before we would bump into each other again in the Village. I simply couldn't believe my eyes. There was Bob Dylan walking down West Fourth Street, by himself. At that moment he was one of the most famous men in the world. Bill Graham maintained he could sell out the Pacific Ocean in three hours by placing a notice in the restroom at Zim's, a popular San Francisco eatery. Bill may have been exaggerating, but not by much. Dylan's fans numbered in the millions and many considered him not only a musical prophet but someone who could chart their individual destinies. This was a hell of a row for anyone to hoe, especially someone like Bob, who had a jumpstart on being paranoid.

It was beautiful to see him out and about without any protection. My wife Bonnie Jean was with me and she and Bob go way back to the University of Minnesota. We had ourselves quite a little reunion right in the middle of Sheridan Square. Bonnie Jean and I were staying just around the block at the apartment of some friends. I was in the process of writing *The Hog Farm and Friends* before heading west for my third spinal fusion. Dylan agreed to stop up and visit, so Bonnie Jean peeled off to straighten the apartment while Bob accompanied me to the corner cigar store for various combustibles.

We hadn't walked half a block when this young, intense, wide-eyed hippie pops up out of nowhere yelling, "Hey man, wait up for a second!"

Bob just sort of shrunk into his shoulder blades.

"No, it can't be!" said the hippie as he cut us off at the pass. "Are you really . . . Wavy Gravy. Well man, I've seen *Woodstock* nine times and I just want to say I really, really admire what you are doing."

I just sort of bit my lip to keep from falling down laughing at Dylan's take on this turn of events.

"I'd like to introduce you to my friend, Bob," I teased.

"Hi, Bob," said the hippie. "But seriously Wavy, I've just got to get your autograph or my girlfriend will never believe me and she's your biggest fan."

"Oh no she isn't," I muttered. "I've got one out west with feathers."

Reflections on Ascension to Flavorhood

Who woulda thought it. In my wildest dreams it never occurred to me that I, Wavy Gravy, would be asked to lend my name to an ice-cream flavor.

That's right, Wavy Gravy Ice Cream. What a concept. One's wildest dreams seem tame indeed next to true-life adventure here at Reality Ranch. Just when you thought it was safe to go back into the freezer. . . . Wavy Gravy *Ice Cream?*

It was hard enough for some people to believe I was *even* a human being—*"What* did you say his name was?"—let alone a frozen dessert. Not just some passing dreamsickle either, but a full-blown Ben & Jerry's superpremium flavor. As it turns out, I have a Brazil-nut base with a caramel swirl and rainforest toffee crunch and chocolate chunks. I am the most politically correct ice cream known to humankind.

And how did this all come about, you may ask? Go ahead. Ask all you want. But don't ask me. Maybe Ben Cohen. That's right. The ice-cream Cohen. Or was it David Harp, the harmonica instructor? David once taught harmonica at Camp Winnarainbow and helped us get a grant from the Ben & Jerry's foundation for our camp scholarship program. It seems most appropriate that any profits I incur in my ascension to flavorhood should go to Winnarainbow.

But stop that future tripping, and don't count the money till it's spent. Let us return to those thrilling days of yesteryear— or was it the year before that? It began to filter into my consciousness that I was being considered to be Wavy Gravy, the food product. At first I didn't take it all that seriously, but that was before I met Ben.

I had just finished sharing some theater games with ghetto kids on the grassy banks of the San Francisco marina, when he and David Harp popped up out of the approaching fog like characters from *Casablanca.* I had helped them network to make an agreement with the Rex Foundation (the charity wing of the Grateful Dead) for the use of Jerry Garcia's name on Ben & Jerry's flavor Cherry Garcia. I was extremely peripheral in this, but Ben thanked me for my involvement and mentioned my possible flavorhood briefly in passing. Phone calls from both him and David Harp began to bring the idea into fruition. An East Coast rendezvous was arranged for the fall.

I was scheduled to teach a course, "Clowning and Compassion," at the Unitarian Conference Center in Rowe, Massachusetts. Ben would pick me up and drive me to my next gig, just outside Worcester. This really blew my mind. The president of the ice-cream company chauffeuring an aging hippieclown from one end of the state to the other just did not compute.

Better still, he brought along his sweet wife, Cindy, and six-month-old daughter, Aretha. I got to ride shotgun in Ben's dusty late-model Saab sedan and spill my whole life story before we got to Barre and the scheduled pit stop at The Insight Meditation Society.

As we drove up, a walking meditation was in progress.

What springs to mind is a scene from *Night of the Living Dead.* Ben was properly flabbergasted, not only by the visuals but the concept of all these people spending three straight months sitting upright and watching their breath.

On our arrival, we were whisked inside, where Aretha got her diapers changed and I delivered an unanticipated (by me) afternoon of clown dharma for the hired help . . . and Ben. It was Bennie and the Breathers, and it was big fun.

By the time they finally dropped me at the Blue Plate for my nighttime gig, I really felt like family. But I couldn't help and wonder if Ben conducted all his interviews at such close quarters. No matter. I had survived his open-heart surgery. It was time to start making ice cream.

In the ensuing months, smoking boxes would arrive at the Hog Farm house, transported in the trembling hands of terrified mail carriers on their appointed rounds. But it was no bomb for these Berkeley anarchists. Only dry ice and innocent ice cream—test batches of Wavy Gravy Ice Cream cloaked in coded containers to confuse the industrial spies. You people probably think I'm kidding.

Then one fine spring afternoon, in walked Ben *and Jerry.* They seemed larger than life, but then, the only other place I saw them together was adorning the pints of their product in our family freezer. We had scheduled a photo shoot in our backyard that afternoon. I was destined to join them on the lid of my flavor, and at their fortieth birthday party in Waterbury, Vermont. I was flown to Vermont by the company Joy Committee. I surprised the birthday boys and addressed the workers at their monthly meeting.

My first appearance was at a breakfast for the night shift, where I shared a quote from Jack Kerouac's *Mexico City Blues:* "Them bacon and them eggs. If you guys only knew how good them bacon and them eggs really was you'd stop writing poetry and dig in!'' I kept it short and sweet, as these folks had worked all night and were a tad laid-back.

The day shift was another story. Almost four hundred strong, they filled the delivery bay with their bodies, and the ethers with their unbridled enthusiasm. I gave them my best shot, complete with bags over the head, clown-drag, and the Funny Mantra. I explained Camp Winnarainbow, so they'd know firsthand the fruit of our collective labor.

These workers share in both the company profits and the knowledge that they are doing good works in the world. This is a whole new way of doing business. Ben and Jerry's gives 7½ percent to charity and the boss can only make five times as much as the lowest-paid employee. Wooga Wooga! This is an evolutionary act and I am proud to be a party to the party. They plan to roll me out in a tie-dyed container. Feel free to eat your heart out.

The Clown by a Nose

Clowns are a fairly recent addition to the historical horizon. They did not kick in big-time until the arrival of the great Joseph Grimaldi in the early 1800s. Grimaldi's Joey was the prototype for all would-be bozos. He brought the clown to the center ring with his major breakthroughs in costume, makeup, and comic genius. There is a famous story about his visit to a psychiatrist in Vienna while in a fit of great depression. Not knowing the identity of his patient, the good doctor said, "You need to take some time off. Go to the circus. Go to the circus and see Grimaldi."

"But I *am* Grimaldi," he moaned.

The word *clown* comes from the native English and means a clod or bumpkin. The red nose first evolved to indicate drunkenness. My own life as a clown began with my acceptance of a red rubber nose. I literally followed my nose into clown-dom. By smearing the inside of my rubber nose with tiger balm, which is a hip form of Vicks, I discovered I could keep my chakras clear and my sinuses open. I once had the pleasure of buying out every red rubber nose in Kansas and Missouri. I passed them out to the under-the-counterculture who had come to protest at the Republican National Convention. We circumnavigated the Republicans in the Kempner Arena and the poor police would not club the clowns on color TV.

Why?

I cannot say this too many times: *Clowns are safe!*

In point of fact, the only time I was physically abused as a clown came about in the following fashion:

It was a cool and foggy morning in the fall of '89. When the phone rang I fell out of bed and staggered dopily toward the instrument of torment at my desk.

"Whozit?" I rasped.

The voice on the other end said excitedly, "Wavy Gravy, I'm real sorry to wake you so early, but the police started moving in and arresting people at dawn, so maybe you could get down here right away."

By the time he had finished the sentence, I was wide awake and mentally getting dressed. An old adrenaline junkie doesn't need much prime.

"I'll be there in a flash," I said, moving swiftly into sweat-suit and sneakers.

The campus police were coming down on about a hundred demonstrators who had been living for about a month on the wide marble steps of Sproul Plaza at the University of California in Berkeley. I was very proud of these young men and women who daily put their bodies on the line to force the university to divest its huge portfolio in South Africa. I was honored to get this phone call.

No time for makeup or giant shoes. Just the basics—valid I.D., nose, bubbles, kazoo—and I'm out the door like a shot. It's a fast five-minute drive from the Hog Farm house to campus. The TAC squad already had the place surrounded. Inside, students and activists were being arrested methodically and taken inside Sproul Hall (re-named Biko Hall by the students). I slapped on my clown nose and walked up to the ominous blue line.

"Excuse me, officer. Could I please get through so I can join my friends?"

"You're too late," said the Man.

"I missed my wake-up," I joked, but the officer simply shut down behind his mirrored eyes. I knew at once I would have to find access elsewhere.

People were being processed inside the hall, then walked out the back door and into waiting buses which, when full, would whisk them off to Santa Rita Prison. I laid under the front wheel of the first bus, which got their attention right away. The captain in charge loomed over me and asked, "Wavy Gravy, what are you doing under that bus?"

"Good morning, Captain. I'd like to be arrested so I can go to jail with my friends," I answered, thrilled to be recognized. *Now* I'd get some results.

"Well, why don't you go around front like everybody else?" he suggested.

"Well sir, I tried that first but they said I was too late so I ran around here to give you the opportunity to tell your grand-children about how you arrested the voice of Woodstock."

He laughed pleasantly enough and said he'd get back to me. I figured he was one of the good cops. Lenny Bruce told me to always give them the benefit of the doubt. You had your pigs, your cops, and your peace officers, and each one's different.

When the bus was full, the captain came over and said, "Okay, Wavy Gravy, you win! Get up. You're under arrest."

"Finally!" I exclaimed, scrambling to my feet.

Well, lightning fast, that sneaky peace officer leaped on the bus, slammed the door, and away they drove—laughing at me sucking in their monoxide on the curb.

Not to be thwarted, I lay down under the wheel of another bus. This time I was joined by legions of protestors who also missed their wake-ups. For us, they brought in the mean and nasties, who approached with batons and brute force. First they ripped off my clown nose and then they threw me about ten feet in the air.

Ouch, it hurt. Those old bones didn't bounce so well anymore. What really ticked me off was that they had to de-clown me first, and only then could they kick my ass. These were old-line campus cops. Down and dirty dinosaurs from those stormy salad-years when Ronald Reagan was governor and everything went like it came.

To add insult to injury, I later discovered that they pinned my nose to the bulletin board at the campus police station. But, the joke's on them. The university has divested, apartheid is almost over, and I have a whole box full of noses.

The Muse Is Loose

I got mine through *The New York Times*. It happened on Wednesday, the third day of April, in the early A.M., amidst my morning marriage of java and journalism. I was directed to page B6 of the Living Arts section. On the upper left-hand corner of the paper my hostess had written, "Wavy, read on." Next to that was the headline "A Conference on Jell-O Learns What's Shaking," by Barbara Gamarekian. It seems that the Smithsonian's Museum of American History had assembled a panel of scholars to discuss "that quivery, shimmery jewel-toned gelatin that Americans have been eating for almost a century. Jell-O."

It was with great joy that I devoured Ms. Gamarekian's detailed account of this tongue-in-quivering-cheek event. I learned that Jell-O was invented by Pearl Bixby Wait in 1897. Like Jesus, Mr. Wait was a carpenter by trade. His wife May thought up the name Jell-O. Just what Mr. Wait was doing with all those hooves, skin, and bones lying around the house was anybody's guess. Least of all the United States government, who don't classify the stuff as an animal product, even though it is made up almost entirely of the aforementioned body parts.

No matter! Jell-O is such jolly stuff that even dour Uncle

Sam cannot resist its irresistible allure. It is to me a healing plasma and a formidable buttress against the slings and arrows of outrageous assholes.

In point of fact, I once suggested the use of a moat full of Jell-O in lieu of hiring a motorcycle gang for security at a major American rock festival. This came in the wake of Woodstock and Altamont so I was taken quite seriously. After many months of correspondence, the conglomerate, General Foods U.S.A., mailed me, Wavy Gravy (Chief of Security, Woodstock Music Festival, Ret.) several cases of Jell-O in various flavors for research and development.

The rock festival was subsequently cancelled and the cases of Jell-O were stored in the underbelly of the bus that was our mobile home (out of sight but never really out of mind).

It was one year later, in the spring of 1970, that we drove our rig into Yellow Springs, Ohio. The Hog Farm was part of a convoy of buses barnstorming across America under the auspices of Warner Brothers, who were filming the darn thing, dreaming of a sequel to Woodstock. Every few days we would stop and set up a stage and our camp of tie-dyed teepees. The studio would then fly in established rock-and-rollers. They would either perform on stage for a limited local audience or accoustically around the campfire for just us hippies.

It was a gorgeous day in Yellow Springs when we pulled into Antioch College and started setting up the stage. Summer school was in full session and perhaps it was a student (or the infamous Thomas King Façade), who procured the companion gun-turret to a World War II B-29 bomber for our edification and amusement. Removed from the Flying Fortress, it resembled a giant clear-plastic dessert dish. The thing cried out for Jell-O.

It was the actualization of a major fantasy to see the great transparent turret chock full of the wiggling, jiggling red stuff.

We moved it center stage and left it gleaming in the midday sun. But wait: those radiant rays were our undoing, reducing a once proud cherry Jell-O to a ruby red soup.

But wait: the addition of an enormous amount of dry ice re-jelled our fantasy and added an additional element of delight. The Jell-O became geothermal, which caused it to shudder uncontrollably, then release a series of smoke-filled bubbles. The bubbles would rise slowly up from the bottom of the bowl. They would dimple the mirrored surface briefly, and then announce their arrival with a distinct and primordial, "BLOOP! BLOOP! BLOOP!"

I vaguely remember holding a microphone up to the bubbles as they burst. BLOOP! BLOOP! BLOOP!

The sheer majesty of this amazing moment inspired the hasty creation of a large banner bearing the slogan "World Peace Through Smoking Jell-O."

We were lost in the crown of our own creation when we heard the sloppy splat of students jumping in the Jell-O. Countless college kids were leaping with lemming-like abandon into the bowl. Its sticky red fluid flew in every direction, coating all and everything in its cheery cherry glaze. The cleanup was a sticky quickie that would haunt us later down the road.

Our next scheduled stop was in Washington, D.C., where we hosted the Alice Cooper Band. The haunting occurred later that night. Alice added a little flair to the finale by shooting a flare heavenward with his trusty flare gun and then, by flare rocket's red glare, Alice proceeded to disembowel a giant pillow. It took a couple of stiff jabs of his rusty trusty trident . . . when the pillow ripped open and filled the air with a rosy fountain of floating feathers.

Ahhhhhh!

I believe it was Dick Tracy's Diet Smith who said, "The nation that controls gravity controls the universe." If only I could have activated Mr. Smith's invention at that moment, thus freezing forever those fickle feathers of fate.

Alas, all we could do was watch them float earthward and adhere to the wires and cables of Alembic Sound Company Wires still sticky with yesterday's Jell-O juice. How surreal it was to spend the next several days plucking the wires clean and cursing Alice Cooper to an eternity in wonderland.

There must be a moral here somewhere. Lenny Bruce once said, "You can't get snot off suede." To this I might add, "Always mop your Jell-O when you drop it or face the sticky feathers of fate."

You may stick that in your *New York Times*.

Hot Smelly Water

This old clown just loves to seek out hot smelly water and submerge. The hotter and smellier the better . . . to a point. The hot pool at Totopani is an excellent example of "too hot for clowns."

Totopani actually means "hot water" in Nepali, and they weren't whistling Dixie. At first glance, it appears innocent enough, steaming away amid poinsettias and pine boughs, with its necklace of snow evoking past yuletide cheer.

Necklace of *snow?* In the summer? Not very likely. On closer inspection the snow was indeed an illusion. A necklace of chicken feathers, to be precise. One has merely to toss an unfortunate chicken into the pool and within a few short minutes the bird can be carefully extracted from the boiling waters, and served as lunch. Had I not hesitated before diving in, I too would have ended up, if not as lunch, then certainly Gravy . . . for the second time in the twentieth century.

The first time was at Spence Springs, just north of Albuquerque in the Jemez Mountains. I was told that Indians would walk a hundred miles in the snow to partake of these healing waters. Spence Springs is naturally nestled near the top of an almost inaccessible cliff, at the base of which roars a stream, which can be crossed by a conveniently felled tree serving as a bridge.

We hit the parking lot at four A.M., parked our buses, and crashed (as in sleep). The entire Hog Farm was stacking z's except me. I decided to go for it. I carefully adjusted my leather and chromium brace under the fierce New Mexico stars and hit the trail for the springs, which was hardly visible in broad daylight. After rolling in the bushes, falling in the brook, and prancing through the prickers, I found the path, and finally was able to hit the surf. "Hallelujah," shouted my mending bones as I immersed myself fully in the hot and healing water. I floundered happy as a clown in this tub of stone until the sun began its morning breakfast of the stars.

All aches and pains had been extinguished when I discovered I was too weak to lift my all-too-feeble frame from out of the broth. I could only cling to the helpful rocks and patiently await my rescue. My skin began to prune and my spine became spaghetti. I was about to assume an advanced state of fluid and say farewell to all I loved, when Jerry Lamb arrived to pull me from the jaws of actual Gravyhood.

Safely tucked into my bed upon the bus I asked my worried wife if someday, should I die, would she cook me up and serve me as Gravy to my friends. It was Country Joe McDonald who first produced the bumper sticker "Legalize Cannibalism," but I was speaking straight from Robert Heinlein's sixties classic, *Stranger in a Strange Land.*

"Not very likely," she replied.

Meanwhile, back in the Himalayas, I have just finished a good soak in the appropriate pool and availed myself of a cold plunge into the Kali Gandaki river as it rumbled on its journey to the Ganges and the sea. This water is glacier-fed, well below bracing on the scale of cold. Only its rapid motion keeps it from achieving ice.

I go back and forth, from hot to cold, until these words no longer define my state of mind and body, which are well beyond all temperature and slightly psychedelic. I rise triumphant from the frozen foam, don my saffron cotton jumpsuit, and hit the trail in quest of grail and rainbows.

The rainbows are the easy part. They dance daily in the sunshine at the junction of two enormous waterfalls just a bit down-river. I get there in a flash and adroitly avoid the ever-present tea shop to seek solace in a tiny Shiva temple at the base of the falls. Here I sit and watch my breath, until my eyes pop open, and in a shaft of sunlight I spy the trail, hewn in solid rock, and heading upward in the general direction of rainbow junction. Up, up, up I travel. Up toward . . . who knows what? I easily reach the pool between waterfalls and leap across to this grassy ledge on the other side. But when I look back, the log I used to spring from had floated over the falls. The only way down was up and it began to rain.

The only way down was up. At first I refused to accept this reality sandwich and waved frantically to the ant-sized denizens of the *chai* shop down below. They had no knowledge of my impending danger and waved back. So I abandoned all hope of rescue from below and began to scale the mountain.

It was hand over hand over hand and fairly smooth for the first half-hour. Then I began to run out of handholds and foot-holds. I was able to climb another fifty yards when I was forced to make a halt and carefully study the situation. I was clinging for dear life to the side of a nearly sheer cliff and had only one chance to continue. I must swing out on this clump of sturdy elephant grass, over this thousand-foot precipice, to reach the next ledge. There lay my only hope—the fresh possibility of proceeding to the summit, and descending down the other side.

I grabbed tightly with my right hand the grass in question, and once again said good-bye to those I loved . . . took a deep breath . . . *and these killer ants ran down my arm and started biting and I somehow flew or windmilled myself both up and sideways to relative safety.*

Looking back, it seems impossible, but who am I to argue? I was the living goof of my own existence, or as Popeye aptly put it, "I yam what I yam!" After another ten minutes of easy upward climbing I reached the top of the waterfall, now gold in the setting sun. When I knelt to kiss the ground in thanksgiving, I found myself staring at four human feet firmly attached to the ankles of an equally startled Tibetan couple engaged in some sort of waterfall worship. They spoke no English and my Tibetan was limited to mantras and momos. The former are syllables of spiritual liberation, the latter dumplings filled with water buffalo or yak.

Then I remembered *namaste.*

"*Namaste, namaste,*" they replied, bowing and smiling.

Namaste means, "I salute the god within you." And we sure did plenty of that!

The couple then led me to their mountain cabin for a good goat dinner and plenty of booze called *chang.* We got pretty rowdy in the wee hours and after a few false starts, they taught me a song in Tibetan.

Then it was my turn, and there in this tiny hut in the high Himalayas, as the sun and moon exchanged command, we sang this Incredible String Band classic:

> *May the long-time sun shine upon you.*
> *All love surround you*
> *and the pure light within you*
> *guide your way on . . .*

Namaste.

Me and
Margaret Mead

"The Hog Farm, eh? I've heard of you. You're that hippie commune," said Dr. Margaret Mead to yours truly. "In fact, I've been studying you. You're nothing new. Haven't you heard of the Mayflower Compact?"

I could only gape in awe at the very idea that I was being studied, along with the rest of my expanded family, by the reigning queen of hands-on anthropology. Who cares if we're "nothing new"? This is big time. I told her there is a quote that makes that very point, and it is located at the very beginning of *The Joy of Cooking*. This is the book we Hog Farmers use to swear on instead of the Bible. It begins with a quote from Goethe's *Faust:*

> *That which thy fathers have bequeathed to thee,*
> *earn it anew if thou wouldst possess it.*

I thanked the good doctor for her insightful observations and went off to join my tribe of hippies. Ah yes, the hip-eye tribe. Same old same old. Peace and love, peace and love.

The Hog Farm commune and a planeload of other folks had been flown to Sweden by the Point Foundation and *The*

Whole Earth Catalog to attend the United Nations Conference on Human Environment in Stockholm in the summer of '72. We were there to help establish and maintain a living example of alternative community. Our community was made up of eco-freaks, indigenous Americans, poets, scientists, assorted Hog Farmers—and Margaret Mead. The Point Foundation not only paid for our flight overseas but floated our 1948 Greyhound, "The Impossible Asp," across the great water. It was to yon transport that I dust repaired.

We were all camped at an abandoned air field in Scarpnack, a distant suburb of the nation's capital. There we established a field kitchen and tent-city to house and accommodate the enormous influx of hippies scheduled to arrive as a result of a poster plastered all over western Europe that pictured U.N. Secretary General U Thant outrageously attired as a member of the Beatles. The poster also carried the banner headline "See you in Woodstockholm."

An article also appeared in *Time,* predicting a great influx, so we *knew* it must be true. So did the Swedish government, who had also read *Time.* When they saw the poster, the government officials promptly sealed their borders to migratory longhairs.

Our contingency was thus limited to ourselves, our occasional guests from the United Nations conference in Stockholm, and six thousand Swedish alcoholics from the large rehab center across the road. In the evening after dinner our sparsely populated model city would fill with our neighbors. We, in turn, would crank up the gorgeous sound system, open up the free stage, and entertain the alcoholics. The Holy Modal Rounders opened the show. They sang songs of "Euphoria" and asked the Fugs' musical question, "Do you like boobs a lot?"

One night I got to moderate a panel discussion on stage

between Paul Erlich and Margaret Mead. I felt like Dick Cavett in deep space. The topic was "Zero Population and the Survival of the Species." During the "Q and A" a nine-year-old girl raised her hand and told the panel, "If what you guys say is true, then my kids can't have any kids." That child's simple statement was followed by the most pregnant of pauses, as each person there realized the urgency of the dilemma that lay before us. That sunny night in Sweden we all pledged in our hearts to work even harder to build a better world.

The opportunity to act arrived the very next day in the person of Joan McKenna. Joan was representing Project Jonah, an organization dedicated to stopping the slaughter of whales before they become extinct. She came by the bus and got us to focus our collective creativity on this issue. In the course of a single afternoon, we covered our Greyhound with huge sheets of black plastic. It soon began to resemble a crusty leviathan. By the end of the day it spouted great plumes of water from its blow hole and could flip the great flukes at its tail.

We then proceeded to drive our bus as a whale, singing and spouting, through downtown Stockholm during the evening rush hour. This piece of theater drove home the plight of the whales to the world press corps. It was a slow news day on the planet Earth, and stories and photos of the whale bus were picked up by wire services everywhere. The next day the U.N. conference passed a resolution against the hunting and killing of certain species of whales that were endangered.

Although I speak of day and night, in point of fact the sun set for only about a half-hour each twenty-four-hour period. This created havoc with our Native American elders and shamen. They would no sooner finish a ceremony to the setting sun than it was time to get up and greet the new day. Great dark bags formed under their eyes and they began to behave in a manner I can only refer to as punchy.

The day before the U.N. conference ended, we attempted to make a strong anti-war statement to the world. This came about in the guise of a giant parade. We marched creatively through the streets of Stockholm, ending up at United Nations Plaza. There we were joined by the U.N. Secretary on the Environment, Maurice Strong, for the reading of our proclamation against the hunting and killing of human beings as an endangered species. This was the first and only time it was suggested during the entire U.N. conference that perhaps war was unecological, or indeed, bad for the environment.

The Secretary of the Environment was moved to tears. The world press, however, couldn't care less. They had already given us our fifteen minutes of fame. The plight of the whales had already bathed in the white impersonal glare of the press. The international media had moved on to other issues.

Twenty years later, the whale population is no longer endangered. Human beings, however, are still awaiting their prime-time salvation.

What Makes Wavy Run

There I was, smack in the middle of a hundred kids. My wife and I co-direct Camp Winnarainbow, a circus and performing arts summer camp five miles north of Laytonville, California. The kids were about to embark on their morning warmups when my wife leaned out the office window and made the now-historic holler, "Dear, the BCA just called, and they want you to run for city council."

BCA stands for Berkeley Citizens Action, an organization slightly to the left of center in the Berkeley political spectrum. The BCA had done a lot of great stuff over the years—implementing rent control, establishing ecological guidelines, creating humane human services, and staying in deep cahoots with Ron Dellums, whom I consider the conscience of the United States Congress.

"Tell them I'll do it if I can run as a clown," I replied as I set off to teach my morning improv class.

Jahanara relayed my reply to the BCA co-chair, Russell Bass. Jah asked if they were ready to endorse a pot-smoking, anarchist hippie clown. Three days later Russell arrived at Camp Winnarainbow. We filled out a forest of forms and drafted my election statement.

Time passed, camp continued, and it was like it never was, except for some extremely existential phone calls with the city clerk as to whether I could be listed on the ballot as: 1) Hugh Romney, 2) Hugh Romney a.k.a. Wavy Gravy, 3) Hugh "Wavy Gravy" Romney, or—my choice—4) Wavy Gravy. This was a bit of an issue as my given name was unknown except to counterculture trivia buffs; the calls continued till Wavy got first billing.

Our poly-tickle meetings took place at the home of Mark and Nancy Gorrel. Mark had run for this same District Five council seat in the previous election. He was extremely qualified and was creamed three-to-one by Shirley Dean. My worthy opponent, Ms. Dean, had been a council member for twelve of the last sixteen years and a citizen of my district for three decades. District Five includes a few scant blocks on the flats, then soars majestically to the crest of the Berkeley Hills. Rare air and big bucks—and they want to keep it that way. I didn't stand a chance.

I forget if I was bummed by this fact, relieved, or a little of both. I saw clearly why BCA wanted me to run against Shirley Dean. They had tried the regular channels and were wiped out. Why not a clown with high name recognition? A chance to shake up Shirley and have a little fun.

By the end of the first meeting our team was in place. I had a campaign manager, Pat McClintock, with deep tracks in Berkeley politics. Dr. Larry Brilliant (Doc Soup) became campaign fundraiser. He provided the necessary dead presidents (Washington, Lincoln, Jackson, et cetera) to grease the campaign trail. Also on the Gravy train were Winnarainbow alumni Mark Portman and Sarah Satterlee, and treasurer Spencer Koffman. I'd never had a treasurer before.

The next day we ordered hundreds of red rubber noses to give out in exchange for campaign contributions. The slogans wrote themselves: "Pick Your Nose," "Just Say Nose," etc. I pasted up and printed our first flyer. Its headline—"Let's Elect a Real Clown for a Change"—was a real attention-grabber. Underneath the photo of yours truly in full clown regalia, I put my full election statement and a plea for fun, funds, and volunteers. To bottom things off, in boldface type: "**Mr. Gravy has a twenty-year commitment to humanitarian and ecological causes. We suspect that Shirley Dean hasn't been to jail once.**"

Our buzzwords and sound bites were both vibrated and bitten. First the Bay Area newspapers and then the FM jocks started chatting up the campaign.

At the same time, we were getting pressure from the straight Left to tone down the fun and play up my *serious* side. It was suggested that I drop this clown thing altogether. Russell Bass of the BCA agreed. I decided then and there to run as an independent. That way people and organizations could endorse me, but not have to wear my nose.

To let the people know there was life beyond Shirley Dean, we decided to focus on voter registration; each day I set up my card table somewhere in the district, signed people up, and passed out noses.

Through my friend at Channel 7, Michael Vosse, we set up an ABC-affiliate interview at my voter registration table, and political publicist Rachael Richmond got me a major interview with *The San Francisco Examiner*.

On October 3, I had my first interview with Dellums's staff to discuss the possibility of endorsement by the congressman. Most of the staffers were familiar with my use of humor and satire to evoke political change. It took two meetings and a lot of soul-searching to win over the Dellums staff.

I got endorsed by Ram Dass, the meditator, and Rusty Schweickert, the astronaut. From innerspace to outerspace, I covered the waterfront. Rachael set up a slew of interviews, including one with Jane Gross of *The New York Times.*

I did almost all my interviews atop Indian Rock, which is just that—a giant rock once frequented by indigenous people, smack in the middle of "my" district. The view is spectacular. You can get a good grasp of the whereabouts of not only my constituency, but of everybody else in the Bay Area. I wanted to project my sense of the interconnectedness that extends far beyond the borders of District Five. I spoke sincerely of my long commitment to helping the homeless, not only in Berkeley, but nationally. Of course, the press all wanted to talk about Woodstock.

Most of the reporters were aware that I was not completely without a political portfolio, having run a pig for the presidency in 1968. In 1972 we ran a rock for that high office, with a roll for vice president. Then along came Nobody, and Nobody is still perfect. From 1976 to the present, I've continued to work for Nobody for President (cuz Nobody is in Washington working for me).

I do spoof presidential politics, but (quoting *The New York Times* quoting me), "Grass-roots representational politics is another thing. It's sacred. Not only would I be compelled to show up at every meeting, I'd be compelled to do a very good job." *The Times* ran a quarter-page article three weeks before Election Day. (They called me "an endearing longshot.") Suddenly I was everywhere. I got a call from a friend who heard about me on a country-and-western station while driving his tractor in rural Nebraska. It was out of control.

Two weeks before the election we finally produced our legendary lawn signs. Designed by R. We Really, a leading exponent of Art Can Be Fun, the flamingo lawn sign was a wonder to behold. Mr. Really and countless campaign co-workers spat out hot-pink, one-legged flamingoes that would vanish like hotcakes later that night.

October 23: Endless European interviews, first *The Economist,* then *The Observer,* then German radio. Relentless German radio. While I was having those last remaining strands of sanity siphoned off, the Wavy Gravy political machine marched on. Pat pulled together a major mailing using postcard reductions of my birthday poster, politically abridged and in full color by Brilliant Color Cards. On the flip side was my election statement and an invitation to my ice-cream social at Live Oak Park on Sunday the 28th.

Ken Kesey had called up and signified he'd show up on Halloween with son-of-the-bus Furthur and his whole shootin' match to help me campaign for city council. I know he had a couple of book fairs in the area, you understand, so I asked what I could do to help him plug his new books. He said the best advertisement was not to mention them at all.

But would he show up? *Never trust a Prankster.* I must prepare for any eventuality. Rachael Richmond jumped on this one with reckless abandon. Invitations went out to every piece of print and electric media on the hemisphere: *Come and Ride the Gravy Train, a Historical Reunion . . .* like the campaign trains of yore. She invoked Franklin Roosevelt, Bobby Kennedy, and the Grateful Dead.

The press didn't need much persuading, and Kesey & Co. showed up *on time.* I immediately went into deep shock and the rest of that afternoon was a bit of a blur. While I waxed psychedelic with Mr. K. from atop Furthur II, Rachael started packing the press into an assortment of vehicles and we wobbled our way out into the afternoon traffic. Motorists pulled over and stared as we pitched anchor at Peet's Coffee, Black Oak Books, and the Juice Bar Collective, got out and pressed some flesh.

A few fast photo ops and we were on the road again, this time stopping at Pegasus Books and the headwaters of Solano Avenue . . . then into the Solano Tunnel and a near-decapitation . . . then left on Spruce and up into Shirley Dean country.

All the while the P.A. was blasting "Hit the Road, Jack," and we be singin' along with Ray, shakin' our rattles and our booties, and the surrounding populace just stared dumbfounded out the picture windows of their million-dollar homes at this full-scale invasion of their avenues. The bus had to shift down into compound low to accommodate the climb up, up, up, into the Berkeley hills. Furthur II's engine was heating up dangerously. It became necessary to abort my somewhat misguided plot to pretend to dose the Berkeley water supply, which lies at the top of the hill.

I must say, I enjoyed hearing Kesey say all those nice things about me to the assembled media. Without clown white, I'm still not blush-proof, even on the evening news. We got major time on all the locals, and seven minutes of CNN.

But the all-time media thrill for me was to end up in living color on the bus with Kesey on the front page of *The San Francisco Examiner*. Kesey must have cut loose a real hooter 'cuz I am frozen forever in total cosmic crackup. What an honor it was to spend Friday the first peeping out of a thousand newspapers vending boxes . . . peering through the plexiglass and filling all who looked back with the possibility that this campaigning stuff could be *fun!* That day we painted some real rainbows on an otherwise gray political landscape.

Pat squeezed in one last mailing, containing the *Times* article and other tidbits—endorsements by Ron Dellums, the East Bay Greens, the Berkeley City Workers, Berkeley Citizens Union, and the League of Conservation Voters. We reprinted one piece from the *Bay Guardian* which included the "F" word, a first for campaign literature. My endorsement included a line from my interview, "If anyone is going to fuck with rent control they're going to have to go over the top of me." I can't believe I actually said that.

My campaign's next gift to Berkeley politics was my ice-cream social—an afternoon of rock-and-roll, short speeches, and free Ben & Jerry's ice cream—on the last Sunday before Election Day. It went off as good as it gets. From noon till dusk by the peace wall in Martin Luther King Jr. Park, just across the street from the old City Hall—sunshine, sweet music, and booths for good causes like Forests Forever, Big Green, Recy-cling, Rent Control, better schools, and so on. This was a real community/family event, with special focus on the kids. We had juggling workshops, face painting, and a whole lotta clowns. It was an ideal non-threatening afternoon for local folks to come and check me out. Pat brought in a medicine woman to bless the day and I talked about how I would like to introduce stuff like aikido and circus skills into the public schools. I had stated earlier that I would throw a pie in the face of any politi-cian who went over five minutes. To show I meant business, I displayed two chocolate creams stage left. This was an ex-tremely effective method of keeping things moving along, and I plan to institute it often in daily life.

The next morning was the "Great Debate" at 7 A.M. on Pacifica radio KPFA, with Chris Welsh moderating. Shirley showed up with her husband, Dan, who is a student adviser in the Berkeley school system. I brought both my noses and a kazoo for back-up. Shirley was focused like a laser. She said she wanted to *fix* Berkeley, as if the city were a giant cat. Potholes, sewers, and speeders are Shirley's main slice. I suggested she think of those potholes as reverse speed bumps, and spend more money dealing with the homeless and the youth . . . and . . . and . . . you've got to remember it was early for clowns and my mind hadn't yet kicked in.

"I've got it, I've got it! A chicken in every pothole . . . that's it!" And then I considered the legions of outraged animal rights activists on my case . . . "Make that a rubber chicken in every pothole."

Holy shit! Shirley Dean just laughed out loud . . . on the radio. This is another historic moment in Berkeley politics. Chris and I are struck dumb, but not Shirley! She is going on about this rubber chicken that was given to her by the BCA at a City Council meeting. It was beautiful to watch this extremely inhibited woman open up like that. In the spirit of the moment Chris encouraged Ms. Dean to reach over "and give Mr. Gravy's rubber clown nose a little squeak." Shirley Dean surrendered to the spontaneity of the moment and gave my proboscis one hell of a squeeze . . . *and the nose refused to squeak,* and it was trauma time on Pacifica. I tried it myself and it worked perfectly, which didn't help anything. But all her defenses were back in place and it was back to politics as usual.

Voting was something of a Zen exercise. The ballot book was a voluminous tome of endless bills and initiatives. Mine was a doorhanger provided by the BCA and featuring, for City Council in District Five, one Hugh "Wavy Gravy" Romney (as it turned out). What a rush it was to plunge into the bin of official decision and cast a ballot in favor of fun.

The rest is history. Shirley Dean got well over four thousand votes and I got just over two thousand. Such a relief! Such a disappointment! I knew from the get-go that it would take an act of divine intervention for me to win this election, but there is a major portion of this sentient dude that lives for such far-fetched opportunities. It's what makes Wavy run.

Sure, I could have done it differently—put my clown in a closet and dressed up in real clothing. I could have compromised my essence and swallowed my soul.

What we did was tickle the political fancy of a nation bored with the usual bill of political fare. That tickle rippled through Europe and ended up on Russian TV, where it was reported that in the United States of America there was a "just and serious" clown running for public office. "Only in California," chortled the commentator.

But, after all, our fair state has spawned an actor president and a tap-dancing senator. Just the other day I read that Sonny Bono was running for the United States Senate.

I may not be out of this yet.

The Psychedelic Solution

"Hello . . . Wavy Gravy? You don't know me but I know everything about you, Hugh. I've read *The Electric Kool-Aid Acid Test* at least five times and the Hog Farm book twice and I really need your help."

I don't remember how many times I've fielded this kind of call. That particular karma keeps running over my dogma again and again. It's always about four A.M. and I am running on automatic.

"You have some Gravy in your ear," I rasp into the receiver.

"Oh, wow. I just knew you were going to say that, man," says the caller. "Oh, Wavy, I am so fucked up. I mean, I took these three hits of acid and I thought I could handle it but . . ."

I can actually deal with this one in my sleep, which is a good thing because at four A.M. I do a pretty good imitation of a sleeping clown.

"Don't worry, it'll wear off before you know it. But to speed up the process I'm going to give you a strange request. This is the official sure-fire solution to your pollution. Are you ready to receive data?"

"You bet I am. Fire away."

"Go out and get a root-beer float."

"What???"

"You heard me," I said. "Go out and get yourself a root-beer float and drink it down. If that doesn't work, call me back."

"Okay man, it sounds pretty weird but I'll give it a shot," says the voice at the other end. "Hey, thanks a lot."

"Don't mention it," I say, hanging up the phone, knowing I can rest easy. For some bizarre reason they never call back. I think that the sheer effort of scoring a root-beer float at four A.M. is just so time consuming and requires so much concentration that it brings you down to where you can deal with the situation at hand.

I took most of my psychotropics publicly in the sixties. Thirty years later my phone is still ringing. I feel a deep obligation to not only pick up the receiver, but to do my very best to help whoever's on the other end. I owe a lot to those early chemical insights, like the irrefutable knowledge of the interconnectedness of all life.

I was a hip comedian with a Packard convertible, a condo on San Francisco Bay, and a beautiful French wife, Elizabeth. I had already recorded two albums and was performing nightly in one of the best improvisational theater companies in the country. I was filled to the very brim with my own self importance. *Hey, Ma—look at me!* I had already taken several "trips." It was *trés* recreational in those days to take a pill and watch the floor move.

On Mondays, the Committee Theater was dark and we had the day off. I would drop some acid and dash about the city having fun. Then one day the stuff really hit me, and I up and dissolved into the universe. I saw immediately how insignificant I was in relation to everything else. I felt like I was a zit on the butt of creation.

At the same time that I began to realize my own potential

godhead, my old mind just dribbled out my ear. I was filled with an overwhelming desire to surrender my life to this amazing energy and let it lead me where it would. I couldn't help myself. So I staggered off into space, leaving my entire scene behind me. In search of God knows what? I felt firsthand that God was real and I wanted to go to work for Him. (Her? It?) Sounds kinda wacky and pretentious, but it was true then and it is still true today. What a long strange trip it is. I wouldn't have it any other way. These days I rarely need the drugs to keep myself on course. Mostly I just breathe and meditate and pray.

I was lucky my mind didn't up and explode in those early psychedelic days. Somehow I always got pure drugs and good advice. Yes, I was very, very lucky. I worry about the youth today, scoring bad dope on street corners and baying at the moon. There must be a better way.

Before criminalization of LSD, the rich people would drop acid with a qualified psychiatrist, who would serve as a guide and lead their clients through all sorts of spiritual experiences. If you had the money, honey, they got the God. The famous photo of Henry Luce, the editor and publisher of *Life,* standing in the garden with his psychiatrist while conducting a bed of daffodils says it all.

Such shaman guides should be available today to lead us and our youth through to the other side and safely back again. That the federal government should keep us from these experiences of true revelation, I feel, is truly criminal.

I tell the kids today to beware of the stuff you score on the street corner. It could blow your mind for good. I think eighteen-year-olds should have legal access to mushrooms and peyote in a controlled environment. The peyote ceremony of the Native American church would make an extraordinary rite of passage into adulthood. (It could be like having a bar mitzvah or first communion, with the drug as sacrament.) With this to look forward to, young people might well forsake the corner connection and wait for their coming of age.

At my kid's camp all drugs are forbidden.

"Ring . . . Ring . . . Ring."

I'd better get that.

"Hello, you've got Gravy in your . . . What's that? All they had was Yoo Hoo!"

Confessions of a Mutant Dove

A smart bomb is one that refuses to explode.
—Wesley "Scoop" Nisker

A movement is when people do all the things they sing about.
—James Bevel

Somewhere in the ancient times (the late sixties or early seventies), I would fantasize aloud into a microphone about assassinating Richard Nixon with a Bic pen. The company ran an ad on national television where they would load a Bic pen into a special gun, shoot it through a board, and then write with it.

"Eat Bic, Dick! It's mightier than the sword!" *Pow!*

Ram Dass talked me out of it. He suggested I learn to love Nixon. What a challenge! Vietnam was playing nightly in the living rooms of America. Wall-to-wall carpet bombing, death and devastation doled out daily in *his* name: Richard Milhous Nixon, sentient being, potential Buddha?

Yes! My sense of humor kicked in and I began to create a shrine to worship Dick. At the corner costume shop I copped a plastic Nixon mask and lit it indirectly so it glowed all goofy in the dark. Sometimes silly is a savior slipping sideways through the horror and evoking peals of healing laughter at the bloody gates of hell.

Now it's 1991 and I find myself beating around the Bush somewhere between Iraq and a hard place called Kuwait. The Berlin Wall has fallen. The Russians were being nifty and it looked like the Defense Department had to get a real job, until Hussein hit the fan. So instead of spending millions at home we tossed millions overseas to make the world safe for other people's automobiles. Certainly not democracy, as Kuwait is ruled by a royal family created by the British in the thirties. The way I understand it, the emir owed Iraq a bundle for fighting Iran and wouldn't cough it up, so Hussein rolled in with his enormous Third World army and annexed the whole damn country—oil wells and all.

This really ticked off Bush and the British, who were Kuwait's main customers. So they got together this whole posse of nations who think Hussein is a despot-bully-schmuck (which he is—no doubt about it), and they slam him right in the national wallet. This is called "sanctions," and is the diplomatic way to force Saddam to get out of Dodge. Well, buckaroos, it seemed to be working too slow to suit Uncle George, so he sorta upped the ante and dumped five hundred thousand troops and all their stuff, like tanks and planes, smack in the middle of the desert. And not just our guys either, but the Brits and a whole lotta Third World countries who had it up to here with Saddam Hussein and missed out on all the recent "good" wars.

So there they were. The U.S. of A. and its coalition partners on one side and half a million Iraqis on the other. We gave 'em till high noon to skedaddle but they just stuck out their tongues and dug in their heels. So with the permission of the United States Congress and the United Nations Security Council, the war to liberate Kuwait began in earnest. Sortie after sortie of aerial bombardment rained down on Iraqi installations in Kuwait and Iraq. A kinder, gentler genocide began through-out the whole theater.

Meanwhile, back in the lobby of the free world, vigils and demonstrations were held from sea to shining sea. It was a mixed bag of Quakers and pacifists, hippies and punks, teach-ers and students, black, white, rich, poor. My wife and son were arrested at the federal building in San Francisco while I par-ticipated in peace rallies in the south and on the east coast. Unlike Vietnam, each rally was flavored with compassion for our troops: "Bring 'em back alive!" "No blood for oil!" "Peace now!" Two hundred thousand gathered in Washington, D.C., with an equal number in San Francisco. Somehow the turnouts were enormously diminished in the popular press as peace became unpatriotic. So hundreds of thousands became tens of thousands in the papers and they were balanced by flag-waving frat houses hooting, "U.S.A.!, U.S.A.!" and, "We're Number One!" followed by gaggles of service wives who successfully tied a yellow ribbon around the all-American psyche. The Super Bowl was an orgy of red, white, and . . . blew me away.

Now you don't have to be Werner Von Braun to know that Wavy Gravy is a world-class, dyed-in-the-wool peacehead. I think killing people is wrong. It's simple: War is a complicated way of getting acquainted and we are all the same person trying to shake hands with ourselves. Once you realize the intercon-nectedness of everything you become a citizen of the planet first and foremost. My planet, right or wrong, and to hell with the marines of Uranus.

Seriously, folks, it got real frustrating to be glued to the CNN scud bowl and circus of surgical strikes (ad nauseam), knowing each antiseptic sortie equaled somebody's darlin' blown to shreds—what was once the crown of creation: a human being. Yes, despite all the dumb Iraqi jokes, they are human beings who are as sacred and holy as you or me.

The successful launching of the ground war with almost negligible American casualties had the antiwar movement in this country demoralized and on the ropes. Demonstrations were often ignored by the media or given brief attention at best, and then back to the flag-draped masses already in progress. Polls gave the president an unheard-of approval rating for his handling of the crisis. Liberals defected in droves to the ranks of warheads. Almost everyone I knew felt helpless and alone. I felt I had to do something positive, in my persona as a spiritual clown, to slip around the barricades. There was a tangible news blackout of peace-movement-related stories imposed upon newspapers and television. This was brought on partly by frightened sponsors and the seeming furor of public opinion.

Eighty-seven percent approval? I'm sorry, I just don't believe those numbers. No one ever asked me or anyone I knew how we felt about anything. Well, it was high time they found out.

I got together with like-minded brothers and sisters in my hometown and we formed the Peace Action Committee. We agreed to work on a public event together called Creating Peace. It was to be held from noon till dusk on a Sunday at the Peace Wall in Martin Luther King Jr. Park in Berkeley. The Peace Wall was the brainchild of Carolyn Marx, who assembled it from thousands of tiles created from as many separate individuals, each containing their dreams for a peaceful world frozen forever in ceramic. More tiles would be fashioned during the event to promote peaceful resolution of the Middle East conflict. We also planned to have sewing machines to the right of the stage to stitch peace flags and banners on the spot. Musicians set to play included the New Riders of the Purple Sage with special guest Merle Saunders, Ogie Yocha, Buffalo Roam, and Country Joe McDonald; Clan Dyken would bring the equipment to solar-power the stage. There would be food booths and information booths for peace groups like Green-peace and Mothers Against War, and tables for letter writing, poster painting, and other joys. At dusk everyone in attendance would form a giant peace sign in a candlelight vigil, illustrated on the flyer by Lee Mars. The pamphlet also promised free Ben & Jerry's Ice Cream and me in a dove suit.

That idea emerged full-blown up the spinal telegraph and exploded into action in the center of my head. "Just another mutant dove for peace, Officer." And how do you cuff a dove, one wonders.

In the spirit of big-time kitchen-synchronicity, Txi Whizz beamed in from Vancouver for a visit and created the basic costume from white clothes already hanging in my closet. That afternoon I copped a pair of plastic chicken feet and molded-rubber eagle beak at the corner toy store.

In its initial debut at a Grateful Dead concert the mutant dove was subjected to endless abuse and ridicule, like "Look at the big white chicken." I then added an olive branch, which the rent-a-cops thought was a weapon. I instantly scaled down the branch and spray-painted the chicken feet a soft non-threatening off-white. My doveness was further accentuated with the addition of a giant peace button upon my snowy breast.

The Berkeley Peace Action Committee met incessantly to prepare for almost any eventuality—except unconditional Iraqi withdrawal from Kuwait, which happened.

Whoopie! Praise God! *A Hum Dalila!* The Gulf war is over! At least it looks like it's over.

We decided to proceed with the event anyhow. After all, the world can always use a little more peace and it could be a true healing for the whole community—plus the chute was already greased. Nothing could have stopped us except a whole lot of rain. Forecasts insisted the sky would be crying on the day of the show. Now, I'm of the old "trust God but tie your camel" school of doing stuff, so I phoned Intents, our teepee, tent, and awning business up north and asked to borrow the Moss tent and a qualified rigger. The answer was affirmative and I promised to split the gas.

Meanwhile, the sky was a blazing blue and if it wasn't for the weather guys we would have never considered the possibility of future inclemency in the environment. Having covered our back door we went about the business of scoring rip-stop nylon for the banners from North Face, Outback, and Sierra Design, and candles from Gaia and Berkeley Surplus. A Meyer sound system was lined up by our stage manager Russ Jennings and the manager of Buffalo Roam, Russell Bass, dealt with tables, booths, and vendors. Keith Cramer was a rock at picking up the loose ends of licensing and permits, and our own Sindi Petti would man the barricades of banners. Chreil sent press releases to the four directions and Gary Spencer put up ten thousand flyers almost single-handed. Joel Selvin touted our event in the *Chronicle*'s Sunday pink section and the *Express* donated an eighth of a page of their paper to peace; and the sun still filled the East Bay firmament.

The weather bureau was now projecting possible showers and it looked like we might get off with only a warning. On the eve of the event I laid a clear plastic ground tarp on the floor of the stage and sped into the city to leaflet a Hot Tuna concert. The night sky was clearing when I came home to sleep.

The next morning began innocently enough with a typical California sunrise, an almost monotonous beauty that has accompanied each day through all these years of drought. With our reservoirs nearly empty and water rationing imminent, it would be wicked to wish for clear skies, but it sure looked like we got lucky.

I loaded up the van and boogied to the venue. Allison, our rigger, was in the early stages of pitching the stage cover when these big black clouds sprang up over the Berkeley hills and it began to rain—lightly at first, with a tentative stop and start, and stop and start some more. We quickly finished staking the Moss tent just in time cuz it started coming in buckets followed by this blinding flash of lightning, and then a thunder chaser that let all the world know that Berkeley was being bombed.

There was nothing to do but slip into my dove suit and take it all in—one breath at a time.

Great balls of hail came hurling from the heavens as I adjusted my beak in the minivan mirror, straightened my tasty white birdfeet, and grabbed a few incidental objects to get me through the afternoon—my Sony portable radio tape deck with optional microphone, some way-cool tapes to feed it should the occasion arise, and always the omnipresent bubbles and kazoo that are the mainstay of the working clown. I was under the tent about ten seconds when somebody stuck Phil Ochs on the box and the Ben & Jerry van pulled onto the tarmac.

It was so cold that the addition of ice cream to the metabolism brought on spastic fits of hypothermia, but it tasted so good I made my shake sync-up to the song.

All sorts of people picked up on our scene as they cruised by with their cars in the rain to see if we had cancelled. Then they'd park their rig and join us under the not-so-very bigtop. Allen Cohen, a great poet and editor of the resurrected *San Francisco Oracle,* arrived with his wife, Ann, a guitar-playing Gypsy goddess. With song and verse they held our attention for nearly an hour, until up stepped David Whitaker to introduce the "Bread Not Bombs" collective with plenty of hot soup, just in time for Country Joe McDonald, who grabbed Ann's guitar and performed a full set for the faithful and the *Daily Cal.* This all happened during one of the day's better downpours.

It kept looking like it might clear up at any moment, which sort of teased the techies into hanging around. My friend Stacy

Samuels, known to the rest of the world as the caped and banjo-banging Captain Forty-Niner Man, boosted our spirits over the hump and into the sweet spontaneity that lives solely in the land of one thing after another. Stacy was joined by his wife Charlotte on fiddle and by Channel 7 on mini-cam. Their correspondent was nattily dressed, had a pleasant baritone voice, asked some inane questions, and refused to come out from under his expensive umbrella. A couple cutaways and he was history, which probably wouldn't repeat itself although he promised to check back throughout the day. Stacy was really rocking now as he led us all into several hundred verses of "Give Peace a Chance" and after every rousing chorus he added, "Everybody's talking 'bout . . ." And I would read a spontaneously selected quotation from a book called *Seeds of Peace:*

> *No peace lies in the future which is not hidden in the present instant.*
> *Take peace.*
> *The gloom of the world is but a shadow:*
> *Behind it, yet within its reach, is joy.*
> *Take joy.*
> —*Fra Viovani, 1513*

or,

> *All truth passes through three stages.*
> *First, it is ridiculed.*
> *Second, it is violently opposed,*
> *Third, it is accepted as being self-evident.*
> —*Schopenhauer*

and my personal favorite:

When shall it be said in any country of the world, my poor are happy; neither ignorance or distress is to be found among them; my jails are empty of prisoners, my streets of beggars; the aged are not in want, the taxes are not oppressive; the rational world is my friend, because I am the friend of its Happiness: when these things can be said, then may that country boast of its constitution and government.

—Thomas Paine

Right on, Tom.

Enter now the Hundredth Monkey Generation with a giant acoustic organ and a working drum set. They are joined by a long-haired stand-up bassist who told some amazing stories till a tiny pig-nosed P.A. fell out of a crowd, which kept changing throughout the afternoon. Clan Dyken was about to prevail on the pig nose when a big-time P.A. materialized to plug into the already-solar-charged batteries they hauled all the way from Nevada City.

Suddenly there was sunshine and full power. We were smoking in the vector—ablaze with the impossible made easy. Clan Dyken played like gods on fire and were joined by John Dawson from the New Riders for a kickass "Panama Red" and ole Merle Saunders with "Built for Comfort." During this whole section of the still-unfolding miracle people quietly created peace tiles at the other end of the tent.

The sunset only added fuel to the raging flames of rock-and-roll and our numbers grew and boogied into dusk. Then we formed that giant peace sign holding candles in the wind. Chanting and singing for the impossible dream.

Just Peace!

The clean-up and clear-out was effortless and impeccable, as we were aided by our invisible ancestors who rejoiced in our tenacity. No, it wasn't no Woodstock but you really had to be there when the heavens unloaded and everybody chanted, "More rain, more rain!

You woulda laughed as hard as we did.

Tooth or Consequences

I often refer to myself as a temple of accumulated error. As a teen-aged beatnik, I gargled with Hoffman's black cherry soda and brushed my teeth with a Snicker's bar. Needless to say, I gnawed my way through the sixties with only six teeth left in my head. They were joined by a rainbow bridge built by Dick Smith, a dentist suggested by Neal Cassady.

I was impressed with anybody who could get their hands in and out of Neal's never-ending tongue-dance unscathed. Dr. Smith had quick hands, a big heart, and a traveling light show. When he overheard me holler, "The only flag I want to salute is a rainbow," he made me the rainbow bridge to augment my actuals. I don't flash 'em all that much. They just sort of lurk beneath my upper lip. I'm already on my second set of rainbows.

The latest installment was built by Dr. Dugan, a sweet, skilled, and somewhat normal dentist from the city of Oakland. He also built me my lowers, which are not colorized yet. My Technicolor top deck is visible only to small children, who say, "Hey, Mister, you've got colored teeth."

So the kids don't get to thinking this is a cool situation, I feel obligated to tell em' my dental life story, sparing nothing.

Not the anguish of the cavity or the probing of the drill. Not the invasion of the Novocaine (I use nitrous only for X rays), or the final flash of the chromium pliers as they expunged my every chopper, except six.

Each tooth had its own terrible tale to tell. By the time we founded Camp Winnarainbow I had the rap down to a science. At the end of our camp orientation session, I would ask the stagehands to bring down all the stage lights, leaving us in total darkness. Then I would call for a tiny pin-spot to illuminate only my mouth. The same mouth that is still busy telling my tawdry tale of toothy terror. This is followed up by actual example. That's when I remove the rainbow bridge and reveal my gaping gums and six slimy stumps.

The sound of the children at the sight of my lonesome molars has not varied by a decibel in the last fifteen years.

"Eeeeeeeeeeeeeeeeiiiioooooooooooooouuuuu!"

To which I reply, "Brush 'em if you got 'em."

Then up come the house lights and off go the campers in quest of their Crest and their floss. I get dozens of letters each year from bewildered parents:

Dear Mr. Gravy,

I don't know what you did to our little Billy but he has been home only a month and he has already worn out three brand-new toothbrushes . . .

And it lasts, this teaching. Ten, fifteen years down the line. In fact, all the way into adulthood they are still brushing away. This is true because that initial take was so powerful they can always conjure up my mouth (and its painful lack of contents) illuminated in their brain. It glows like a medieval visitation of the holy virgin.

This is the temple of accumulated error in action. In the last fifteen years I'm sure I have reached over five thousand children personally—by word of mouth.

In the far and distant future I may ascend to dental deity. St. Hugh of the suffering stumps. It would be a small price to pay for a world without cavities. Think of it: a world without dentists . . .

Yes, anything is possible if we would only share our errors with others. Come, let us flaunt our fallacies into oblivion.

I say, "Oblivion or bust." And truer words were never spoken.

How I Passed the Acid Test

Return with me now to those thrilling days of yesteryear. Journey back, back—smack dab into the middle of the sixties. My wife for life and I are living in Los Angeles, where we are working together on our first public event, the Lord Richard Buckley Memorial Sunset.

Lord Buckley was a master monologist from the 1950s who left behind a rich legacy of incredible albums recorded on World Pacific, which was also my first record company. Jim Dixon, who had recorded live all of Buckley's material, was also my engineer and record producer. Wisely, Jim didn't turn me onto His Lordship until after my own album was in the can. To observe firsthand my cosmic debt to this great man, we planned this special sunset celebration.

Sweet swinging invitations replete with most cool maps to Moonfire mountain were mailed with this most beauteous chip off the old Buck:

"The flowers, yes, the flowers . . . but the people,
The people are the true flower . . . and it has
been a pleasure to have momentarily strolled in
your garden."

Our L.A. Lemon Grove Street house is abuzz with preparation. Great vats of Bonnie Jean's famous pineapple chili simmer on the stove as the eve of our event approacheth and the rains doth begin in earnest. First comes a trickle and then a torrent. The proverbial cats and dogs rain the night away as the phone rings off the hook.

"Hey man, what about the sunset?"

"Well, let's see what it's like in the morning," sez I, giving my stock reply. I am already semi-somnambulated. After fielding a few hundred calls I unplug the phone and go into full somnambulation.

Come sunrise the sky is still crying as I stagger downstairs seeking my morning jumpstart of java. Imagine my surprise when I enter the kitchen and discover fifty people in Day-Glo clothes, cooking eggs.

The Merry Pranksters and the Grateful Dead had arrived at our house. They were scheduled to appear at the Unitarian Church in the Valley that very evening with their traveling road show. It was a little something entitled Can You Pass the Acid Test?

Our house guest, one Tiny Tim (the same), is beside himself as he describes how Neal Cassady and Ann Murphy had pounded on his door at three o'clock in the morning demanding some grass.

"And they were standing on a whole lawnful," sez the mystified Mr. Tim.

Outside the rain falls falls falls, and inside the phone rings rings rings until finally I freak.

"Call Off The Sunset!"

I tell everyone who calls to meet us at the Unitarian Church in the Valley.

"Some friends of mine called the Merry Pranksters and a

band called the Grateful Dead are doing a little something called Can You Pass the Acid Test? I got to do a couple acid tests back in the bay area and it's pretty cosmic. Yes, we'll all be there and I'm sure it will be wonderful."

At five in the afternoon I begin to get antsy. It is still pouring outside.

At five in the afternoon, the Hassler, Ron Bivert, easily detects my dilemma.

"You really want to go up there, don't you?"

"You betcha!"

At five in the afternoon, several of us float out to the Prankster's rent-a-Valiant moored by the curb and take off for Topanga Canyon, Lord Richard Buckley, and the elusive sunset.

Moonfire Mountain is owned by Louis Beach Marvin III, the eccentric former heir to S & H Green Stamps. Louie had lent me his mountain for this ex-event. We slither the car to a stop at the access road and begin our ascent. After slip-sliding past the ominous metal sign POLICE DOG TRAINING COURSE (which is a ruse), we plod ever upward. A couple of bends later, we hit the summit. That mountaintop is southern California's answer to Sugarloaf in Rio. The view is a gasper.

The moment we arrive the rain stops and the sun sets. And it is a mighty sunset. It is so sensational, I feel ashamed. Here, Lord Buckley and the sun do a glorious golden dance and I have flat-out cancelled their performance due to a little inclement weather. Shame on me.

Never again, I promise. In the entire twenty-five-year history of what is to become the Hog Farm commune we never, ever cancel another public event. Through rain and snow and wind and sleet. Sometimes there is only us and the mail and the hail, but we are that much richer for being there.

COULD WE HAVE THE NEXT SLIDE, PLEASE?

Oh yes, the Acid Test in the Valley. It is a wonderful big success except somebody burns the pineapple chili. Then they flush the charred remains of the stuff down a Unitarian toilet. This plugs up the sewage system for the entire complex, which grinds to a standstill.

WHEN DID YOU ACTUALLY PASS THE ACID TEST?

I would have to say that didn't happen until the Watts Acid Test. This was held about two weeks later.

It is the eve of Lincoln's Birthday, and the city of Watts is still smoldering from recent race riots. Somehow it is cosmically appropriate for the Merry Pranksters to rent this giant warehouse amid those smouldering embers.

Word is out, and most every hip person in southern California shows up. The Dead and all the Pranksters (minus of course, the elusive Mr. Kesey, who is on the proverbial lam) are present and accounted for. These people could make the walls melt and the floor change color for a dollar at the door.

> Get your free legal LSD . . .
> . . . but only until midnight. The law will change
> the very next day.
> So come one, come all,
> come every freak in the free world who can
> scam the transport.
> And let the acid test begin.

The venue itself is this enormous warehouse stretching almost out of sight in four directions. Scaffolding and speakers are stacked everywhere. (Owsley calls this current incarnation "Supersound.") Great metal mounds of microphones and every form of projector, amp, and dimmer—and it is all plugged into itself.

On stage: The Grateful Dead.

At the door: Two brand-new galvanized garbage cans of ice-cold Kool-Aid. One can is also full of LSD-25. About one hundred micrograms a swallow.

The LAPD are standing all over the place, so the situation calls for a little tact. I grab a live mike and cleverly clarify the scene:

"The Kool-Aid in the ashcan on the left is for the kids, and the Kool-Aid in the ashcan on the right is the electric Kool-Aid. Get it?"

Okay, once again: "The ashcan on the left. . . ."

But after dancing for a couple hours to the Dead, a body do get thirsty and seeks a little something wet; and something wet is often three hundred micrograms a gulp.

Pretty soon nearly everything starts to melt down. First the walls, then the people.

"Who Cares?" I hear some sister scream. And Ken Babbs connects her up to Supersound!

"Who cares!?" comes crashing into the collective DNA of everybody in the warehouse.

"Who Cares?" she screams.

And I remember *somehow* crawling to an open microphone.

"Who Cares?" she screams again.

"Some sister has just unglued," I say into the P.A., "and if you care about her, I'll meet you where she is and maybe we can all try to glue her back together."

It takes me maybe twenty minutes of crawling around the place in mid-meltdown till I find this little alcove, slide inside, and there she is . . . the Who Cares girl in all her glory. I crawl over and complete this circle of loving, caring strangers that surround her—and then she turns into jewels and light. And *we* turned into jewels and light.

And that's when I passed the acid test. You understand, when you get to the very bottom of the human soul—to the place where the nit slams up against the grit and you're sinking pretty bad—somehow you manage to reach down and help someone who is sinking worse than you are. Well, that's when everybody gets high and you don't need any LSD and you don't need any jewels or light. Jesus and the Buddha were right!

All you need is . . . love.

Unconditional love.

Janis's Last Laugh

When we got the word that Janis Joplin had died I was in transit with my expanded family. We were temporarily encamped in two painted buses and a tie-dyed teepee somewhere on the inskirts of Amsterdam. The caravan would soon head overland to India, Pakistan, and Nepal. At that moment, however, we weren't going anywhere. Except, perhaps, down in the dumps. Janis had died of a heroin overdose. She was an infrequent user who was given some uncut smack as a favor. Some favor—a free ticket to the sleep that rots. What a waste. What a cryin' shame.

Janis Joplin was never a junkie. She lived life with a passion, absorbed every bump, and sang about it—for her supper and her peace of mind. She could also erupt with great joy from just living in the moment. She was Madame Joy. As such, Janis Joplin had been a living lesson for us all.

She wouldn't like all this moping about.

Perhaps something a little more creative. The flyer all but wrote itself: "Come say farewell to Janis . . . party at sunset in the tie-dyed teepee on Zeeburgerdike." The invitation cascaded through the hippies of Holland like a ball and chain.

I remember the light before sunset was coming alive with

the color of the day. I had sent Fred the Fed out for the Dutch counterpoint to Southern Comfort and he returned with two giant bottles of fermented pine-needle extract. Just in time. The blood-red sun tore up the tulips and set the bricks ablaze. A raggle-taggle stream of hippies poured into the teepee. I particularly remember Peter Pussydog standing there in a Sergeant Pepper jacket with candles blazing on the epaulets.

Someone had placed two perfect *Amanita Muscaria* mushrooms in the pine-needle booze for corks. My, my. My father's mush has many rooms.

So there we all sat, in a sacred circle. We then commenced to eat the corks and pass around the comfort. With each individual swallow we re-remembered Janis. (A warning to the reader: don't try this at home—the Amanita can be fatal if not prepared properly.)

When or how we first met is still a mystery. She was always real glad to see me, though, and would stop whatever she was up to and give me a big warm hug and a slug of whatever she was drinking at the moment. I could make her laugh just by being there. Actually it was more of a cackle than a laugh, deep and delightfully demented like water over rocks just before the rapids. Like her tag on "Mercedes Benz."

Once in the United States of Chicago she took ten minutes out of her concert time to plug the Conspiracy Stomp, a benefit I was doing to raise money for the Chicago Eight. She stomped her foot down in the footlights and declared, "If they are guilty, we're all guilty." Janis went on and on until she felt her audience was honor-bound to attend the stomp.

The following week found us both at the Orlando Pop Festival, where she blew me public kisses from the stage. I just loved her for that. It was a dank cold night in a swamp in the middle of the Okefenokee. At one point the sheriffs had me tell the crowd to burn the bleachers just to keep warm.

During her set, Janis made her own kind of fire and lured Johnny Winter out on stage to add a few licks to the flames. It was when she was dry-humping Johnny that she acknowledged me over the microphone and blew those infamous kisses. I was blushing madly on that dark and muddy night. . . .

When suddenly I was back in that teepee in Holland and it was my turn to swallow again. Somehow without speaking we all knew to hold that last swallow in our mouths, each one of us around the circle, and with great reverence simultaneously spat our final swallows into the fire pit.

There was a blinding flash of flames, and I swear I heard her cackle coming through the smoke flaps.

It Only Hurts When I Don't Laugh

Laughter is just God's gift of audible grease designed to help us humans slip swiftly twixt yon rock and hard place. Whoosh!

All through my life I have attempted to turn adversity into an ally. And chaos into a comedy. Sometimes I succeeded in spades.

Witness the nearly six years I spent bouncing in and out of the clutches of western medicine. Although I attained a certain celebrity as a semiprofessional invalid, it was not all sunglasses and autographs.

Let us begin with my initial spinal surgery in the summer of '68. I became the first patient in the history of Bryn Mawr hospital to wheel his (or her) own gurney into the operating room, leap up on the table, and holler, "Let's Go For It, Docs!"

In less than two years I would be back for a rerun, a little less anxious to jump on the table. I knew what it was to surrender my spine to the scalpel. This time I received a fusion of my third and fourth lumbars. Oh boy! I could hardly wait to get outta the hospital but I didn't have any choice in the matter. They don't call us patients for nothing.

First thing I do whenever I check into a hospital is to decorate. I start off with tie-dyed sheets and a little puja table (or altar), where I always arrange my reminders of Heaven. A candle, some incense, and statues of Buddha, Jesus Christ, and Donald Duck. All my chrome bedguards are entwined with fake vines and artificial flowers. I try to make the hospital a fun place to be in.

One night a new nurse came into my room about dawn and just went crazy. She let out a long piercing scream and went careening down the hallway in quest of the intern on duty. It seems this was her first encounter with tie-dyed sheets and she thought I had bled funny.

My second surgery was also held at Bryn Mawr—this time on April Fool's Day—and it went off without a hitch. I merely turned into my usual mixed marriage of Mr. Potatohead at the mercy of Peter Pain, the lovable green demon on the Ben Gay bottle.

Mr. Pain was having his merry way with me and the nasty nurse on duty wouldn't give me my Demerol. She said it was too early for my pain medicine and that I wanted it too much. The nurse also told me to stop watching the clock. She said I should watch some nice TV instead. Sure, easy for her to say.

Then the potato parted and the proverbial lightbulb flashed briefly on my frontal lobe. I had all signs of any form of chronometer removed from my room. When there was no clock for me to watch, I climbed once again into the cathode's cheery glow. TV Guide became my co-pilot and my savior. All I needed to do was to note the program in progress and check TV Guide. That way I was always on time for my drugs.

After that it was all smooth sailing until I became addicted. Not to the drugs, but television. I learned to practically live inside the television set. I just loved the old movies and in time I became something of an expert on "what's on." I would deeply ponder all the possibilities in *TV Guide* and make elaborate notes in the margins. Over time, friends would phone me up from all over the country for tips on what to watch. They didn't call only for TV Guidance but for other stuff too. Like . . . "How to Survive in the Hospital."

Here is the first simple tip: earplugs are a vital piece of equipment. Never check into a hospital without either earplugs or earphones. That way you are able to control the sounds inside your own head. No more screams and mutters echoing eternally in the hallways of health. No sir, not for me. I just lay there and watch living "General Hospital" with a soundtrack supplied by Thelonious Monk.

On April Fools' night they encased me in plaster from my nipples to my knees. We painted it blue and covered it over with stars. We called our creation Wavy Gravy and His All-Star Cast. Just roll me across the stage, take the money, and run . . . from the phone company. They had been following us forever in a valiant attempt to collect for the countless credit-card calls made by anonymous Hog Farmers and billed to the Pentagon. Erstwhile investigators over the years received sketchy information about a series of calls made by a mysterious caravan of painted buses that never stopped moving. Still, they continued their query until finally, somebody squealed. I think it was my mom.

Their very next call was to my bedside, and was screened by my wife. They had my number this time, and my number was up. They suggested I would be jailed upon my discharge from the hospital. Well, we got a friendly doctor to sign me an early release. My family smuggled me out on a gurney, hidden under a plain white sheet.

My final spinal fusion was performed at San Francisco's prodigious Pacific Presbyterian Hospital in 1972. Dr. Donald

King conducting. Dr King had invented the King procedure, which was then the cutting edge of the craft.

Dr. Larry Brilliant tactfully tried to persuade the kindly surgeon to please perform his procedure.

> DR. KING: *"Do you expect me to operate on this lunatic?"*
> DR. BRILLIANT: *"Meat's meat."*

The clincher came when Herb Caen, the *San Francisco Chronicle*'s dapper rapper of what's what and who's who, printed in his morning column that he would like to meet Jane Fonda, Chou En-Lai . . . and me.

"Well, if Herb Caen wants to meet him, that's good enough for me," was Dr. King's response. Dr. Larry got to scrub up and attend my operation. Thus positioned, he was able to field the occasional flying fragment of my lower back and slip it in his pocket. These grizzly trinkets were subsequently transformed into earrings by hardcore Hog Farmers.

I was transformed into a coffee table by Dr. King. This was the time we covered my full body cast with money from all over the world. We called our creation the Cast of Thousands.

I stuck my tummy out a little extra when they applied the plaster so when I chose to suck it in (my tummy) there was room for a couple ounces of marajahoochie (pot, reefer, grass). I was the stash. This helped to assure me of continuous company in my coffee-table incarnation and I was unbustable without a buzz saw.

As all I could do for a while was lie there, people would plop all sorts of silly stuff on my stomach—ashtrays, coffee cups, and the latest *Rolling Stone*. I also moored babies and gave a great foot rub.

After the hospital, we all moved to Pacific High School, a

geodesic alternative school set in the Santa Cruz mountains. A portion of the property was rented for my recuperation by David Crosby. There was room at Pacific High for my whole expanded family to relax and watch me go cuckoo.

I was attempting to mimic the silver surfer and ride out my pain like a giant wave . . . sometimes successfully. Other times, wipe out and look out, old clown fall down, go boom!

And then I discovered the radio. A simple AM/FM portable model with a reasonable antenna enabled me to achieve an almost out-of-body experience. I found that I could become one with the station selector and go *inside* the radio and find a certain song or a particular artist. Not every time but enough to be spooky. I could also spin the dial at random and the radio would answer me, a la the *I Ching*.

During those long winter evenings after dinner I would lie back in my Cast of Thousands with the radio mounted comfortably on my belly. I had a stethoscope taped securely to the speaker and running into my ears. (This was before Walkman.) I would take requests from family and friends on a piece of paper, then disappear *inside* the radio to honor same.

The results were occasionally miraculous, and at least interesting enough to keep me occupied and pain-free—however, not to the extent that I would consider the prospect of a lifetime in Radioland.

COULD WE HAVE THE NEXT SLIDE, PLEASE?

A Piece on Garbage

Having decided to write a piece on garbage, I tentatively approached the typewriter pondering the possibilities, and be it by magic or sheer coincidence I opened the latest *Whole Earth Review* (Spring 91) to page ninety-four and an excellent article by long-term contributor Sparrow entitled "Garbage in Mind." This simple blast of homespun kitchen-synchronicity might detract a less accustomed mind. My own interest merely peaked around the present to a past well paved with cosmic connections. Witness: the yarmulke Lenny Bruce gave me the day before he died.

We were out by his pool, high in the Hollywood hills. I was rather raw and ranting from a recent acid trip and he was the keeper of the Law. Lenny really loved the Law. He elevated it to something sacred. I thought the Law treated Lenny Bruce like shit. Lenny laid the shit on the assholes who interpreted it.

We had a deal going, Lenny and I. A half hour of Law for a half hour of light. On what would prove to be the last day of our little deal, the clouds hung like hungry lions over the tinseled hills. Lenny Bruce looked me straight in the eye and said, "There is no death." This came from extremely out of nowhere. I had just listened to twenty-nine minutes of lawyers,

D.A.s, and prurient interest—I heard it from him all the time. When John Kennedy was shot I was out at the Los Angeles Law Library copying futz and putz for Lenny's court brief. But, "There is no death!" Now that was one of my lines.

Then Lenny handed me this yarmulke to go inside my hat. I had this ratty old cowboy hat that allegedly belonged to Tom Mix. He said I should sew the yarmulke inside the cowboy hat, so when I took it off I could say, "Howdy Goyim!"

The next day Lenny Bruce was dead. He was cremated at Weinstein's mortuary. I should know. Its name and address were written inside the yarmulke: SOUVENIR OF WEINSTEIN'S MORTUARY. (Dada dada, dada dada . . . Theme from the *Twilight Zone*.)

I wore that hat in the Woodstock film, so it lives forever on the silver screen. "Howdy, Goyim."

In real life somebody ripped it off at a Peace and Freedom rally. Stuff comes. Stuff goes. That is the way of stuff.

Most stuff ends up as somebody's garbage. I immediately read "Garbage in Mind" (remember that article by Sparrow?) and pulled out everything that lit up for me. Some people may call this plagiarism but to me it smacks more of osmosis or religion.

Sparrow says he only reads the magazines that he finds in the garbage. Out of same he has composed an amazing symphony of bizarre facts.

He also says, "I see the garbage as an oracle, like the *I Ching.*" When he was with William Burroughs at the Naropa Institute, Sparrow was assigned to cut up newspaper articles and randomly reassemble them, on the theory that if you cut apart the present, the future leaks out.

Now I'm starting to buzz.

The great collagist Kurt Schwitters proclaimed, "My palate is the wastebasket of the world." Right on, Kurt! But let's don't limit ourselves to the printed page. I once found a glass eye cleaning up after a Grateful Dead concert in those heady Prankster days. In fact, it was Neal Cassady himself who taught me how to read the garbage like a fortune cookie. It's absolutely mind blowing what you can find lying around on the ground these days.

This somewhat esoteric insight became a weekly column that I created for the *L.A. Free Press* called Cream (before the rock band). Cream is what we screamed when all the hairs on our arms leaped up to rigid attention at the sight of something weird. I cooked up my Cream column from a pile of old or new photographs, selected at random, and then animated them by using speech balloons clipped from countless comic books. The balloons were placed appropriately, after their equally random selection. I'd draw them from out of a whole bagful with my eyes closed. Then I'd stick them to the photos. Sooner or later the cream would rise, and the weirder paste-ups would be published in the paper.

Eventually I took the whole thing on the road. It was billed as "Hugh Romney and His Electric Toothpick" and featured me armed with an opaque projector, a pile of weird photographs, and a bag full of bubbles gleaned from countless comic books. Before a live audience I would first beam a photo on the screen, swiftly followed by the addition of random balloons. If the crowd cried "Cream!" I'd glue it all down on camera with a generous dollop of rubber cement.

One evening, for a variation, I reached out and grabbed the snacks right off the plate of this couple sitting ringside and projected them up on the screen. So here we have this enormous Fig Newton telling this Oreo cookie, "Well, Tom, you better git on up de ribber 'fore de natives come and eat you up." This was way beyond the capacity of my brain to contain at that particular moment in time. For whatever reason, it simply got too weird, so I unplugged my machine and returned to the relative safety of the printed page.

My high regard for selective paper was developed in the following fashion. My good friend and occasional roommate, John Gardener Brent, traveled the length and breadth of this land with ten steamer trunks full of amazing paper. When we would move into new digs, vast quantities of the stuff would be used to adorn bare walls with his wonderful weirdness. Each piece was anchored in place by four thumbtacks. With every major temperature change the wood in the walls would expand or contract. This action would propel the tacks out of the wall and create landmines all over the floor we traveled to the toilet. To avoid painful puncture and humiliation, we learned to walk in the dark in a very special way. This technique has served me well in my later life as a soldier of the spontaneous. It's all in the curl of the toe and the arch to the foot as it explores unknown vistas of linoleum. In this mystic manner I acquired all my knowledge of traveling through the world with relative safety.

John Brent was one of the great wits and wastes of my generation. He was also a terrific teacher. On my twenty-eighth birthday he had me lie down on the living room floor with my eyes closed while he proceeded to dump all ten steamer trunks of paper on my head. What a gift. I was allowed to roll in it for hours. Photos of everyone and everything. Layer upon layer of all our lives. All the stuff that ever graced a printed page. I got out my projector and every handful was cream for the ceiling. It was almost too much to bear.

Ten years earlier, John and I had co-directed the poetry readings at the Gaslight Café on Macdougal Street in the Village. We were intense young poets then. One day he whispered to me on a page, "You would not know my skull amid a field of skulls." To which I answered, "The flowers of your skull are budding in the valleys of my open palm."

Ah, youth. John Brent died around 1985 of almost-natural causes. He was my best friend in the whole wide world. I'll bet he left some incredible garbage. And not just paper either: John had an eye for the hard stuff.

Talk about your angels in the architecture. Both John Brent and Lenny Bruce really loved the angels. Also satyrs, nymphs, and gargoyles. They had an eye for the kind of furniture that made sense only in Las Vegas or after a couple of hits of DMT. Dimethyl triptimate was developed by the United States government to spray on our enemies. I think they stopped making the stuff when they discovered a large segment of their test subjects lining up for seconds. Hippie scientists rediscovered the recipe and mixed up a substantial batch, which was absorbed on mint leaves and set loose upon the scene. All perfectly legal in the early sixties. After all, what fiend would find fault with the sharing of a little nerve gas between consenting adults?

I scored a sampler of the stuff and left a taste for Lenny on the bureau of his room at the Swiss American Hotel—with a note wherein I suggested he smoke the mint leaves "until the jewels fall out of your eyes."

Lenny stopped back at the hotel to catch a breather between his sets at the Off Broadway in San Francisco's North Beach section. He was accompanied by his buddy and long-time traveling companion Eric Miller. Eric was a black hipster who also played backup guitar on some of the schtick. They read my little note and went straight for the jewels.

Now, through all his life, Lenny Bruce once told me, he only saw things in black and white and shades of gray. No color, ever—until *kerpow!* Needless to say, when face to face with a full spectrum, Lenny became mega-grooved and super animated. He began hopping wildly around the hotel room. He was Nijinsky on nerve gas, leaping this way and that. While momentarily perched on the window ledge, Lenny accidentally fell over backwards, and out the window of the hotel.

In midair, he called up to Eric Miller (and the gods of circumstance), "Man shall rise above the rule!" Then he hit the concrete with a sickening thud.

I told the doctors at the hospital that Lenny was my uncle, so they let me visit for a minute before they set his leg. "Don't feel bad, it was worth it," he said.

I acquiesced in an instant for, after all, he did get to deliver the most awesome line ever uttered in midair. I foresee a time in the enlightened future when jumping parachutists will cease to scream "Geronimo." Someday, "Man shall rise above the rule" will suffice.

For Whom the Toll Knolls

One sweet September afternoon I visited the expanded family plot. Our official Hog Farm graveyard is located just outside Laytonville at the Black Oak Ranch on a nifty knoll overlooking the earthy brown waters of Lake Veronica and the Winnarainbow waterslide. The green-bearded black oaks share sun and soil with sleek and rusty manzanitas, not to mention the Wilson brothers, and Danny and Butch and Sean and Bud. Sean, Bud, and the brothers are actually interred in bone and ash. The others are represented by their backstage laminates, which sway from branches in the trees.

The wind-chime announces my arrival.

"Company!" Only a whisper of wind on warm grass.

"What's blue and goes ding-dong?"

Not the blazing blue sky haunted by Kamp Kopters, or blackbirds with red wings (also blazing) . . . but, "The Avon lady at the North Pole!"

"Ding Dong!" The wind chimed in and I knew I was not alone.

For openers there were those Wilson boys. They drove their stagecoach and an anonymous passenger straight into our knoll in 1869. Some say they bit the bullets of the notorious

Black Bart. The Wilsons and John Doe came with the property, complete with two moldy marble headstones and one very important precedent.

When three or more are buried in anybody's name, you got yourself a bona fide bone orchard. We have a legal grave-yard. A sacred spot on our own land to plant our loved ones.

And not a moment too soon, cuz we had just lost Sean Cassidy, our very own super-mechanic, bus driver, bon vivant, and substance abuser extraordinare. Sean had just successfully completed an exhaustive detox and decided to celebrate. Whoops . . . our first customer.

Sean's overdose rocked the Hog Farm reality. He left behind a loyal wife and three teen-age boys without an old man to grow old with. He left us Hog Farmers with a total sense of failure, as if somehow we had erred in our frenzied attempt to rehabilitate our brother.

When the news of Sean's O.D. caught up with us, we were in mid-babysit for the children of the Grateful Dead at the Oakland Coliseum. Bob Barsotti somehow got us the keys to the stadium. This is the cathedral of Bay Area baseball, and it was both idle and available.

Friends and family made a large circle in left field where, as the spirit moved us, we expressed aloud our shock and our sorrow. I remember quoting some long-dead Arab who suggested, "Fate is like a kick from a blind camel. If it's a hit, you're dead; if it's a miss you live until you're senile!" There was a good deal of good grief in that left-field circle and a lot of anger with no place to go but home plate.

There was a viewing that evening at a funeral home in Oakland. The next day we brought Sean's body home to Laytonville, where we legally buried him like a Mahatma. We were not just burying Sean. We were burying all our brothers and sisters who—accidentally or on purpose—slipped into the sleep that rots as a result of deadly white powders and booze.

Please God, not another generation. Let them *get it* once and for all. HIGH ENOUGH IS DEAD . . . and I think they got it this time, as I eyeballed each and every teen-ager through the fine words and farewell flowers. I could see a healthy hardness submerged below the tear line.

Years pass and our knoll tolls again. It unknowingly buried our bus driver Butch before we bought the land. Then came Danny Schoffman in his absolute prime. He had just returned from the tropics to say hi—and to get high. He snuck into some smack and never came back. . . . Once again came the shock. Once again came the pain and we added another name on the knoll. I watched our kids take this one all the way in and I saw them decide if Danny's death was to have any meaning they must forever forswear any contact with hard drugs (i.e., cocaine, speed, heroin).

Those rough reminders are on some kinda roll. This year it was Bud whose ashes we buried at the family reunion. We buried him head to head with Sean Cassidy. It was a spontaneous ceremony of song stories and the selection of stones for a kiln.

The ritual helped transcend the pain (always in a circle). And then came the passing of Bud in a bag to the left (always the left). This circle scene is often both humorous and holy. (And it's different every time.)

That's how to keep your ritual rich. You must first realize you are also burying yourselves. We get better and better at that final farewell.

"Hey, we'll miss you guys but we're gonna move on. Who knows when that blind camel's gonna kick again."

After all, we're hovering on the cusp of natural causes. My own father passed away during the writing of this piece. Hugh Romney, Sr., was eighty-three years old and the previous summer had mastered the waterslide. He lived a rich full life as a practicing architect, and designed our Camp Winnarainbow kitchen. When his ashes arrive I'll proudly help him take one more ride down the waterslide before the peace of resting in our knoll.

Meanwhile, if I could muster all my accidentally dead and famous friends for one final benefit boogie we could sell out Madison Square Garden for a month. All proceeds would go to stop that major killer—dysentery. So many fragile sentient creatures dehydrate and disappear out their own asshole.

I'd call the show No Shit and open with Jimi Hendrix and Janis Joplin. Who's on next? There are so many senseless early exits to select from: Paul Butterfield, Mike Bloomfield, Tim Hardin, Richard Manual, almost all the keyboard players for the Grateful Dead. How 'bout Lenny Bruce and Abbie Hoffman for a little comic relief? Good grief! What a show!

Backstage, Hog Farm laminates for the departed hang like autumn leaves on their graveside limbs and rattle for some rock-and-roll beyond our human ears.

Rex,
the Wonder Dog

Rex the Wonder Dog came into my life like a comet hurtling out of the brisk blue sky. We, being the Hog Farm commune in a caravan of buses, were all packed up and ready to leave the rent-free farm in Narrowsburg, New York, bound for New Mexico and a new life, when this ancient, drool-encrusted basset hound fell out of said sky and landed at my feet. I quickly deduced that he became airborne as the direct result of his failing to stare down the Mack truck that just blew by our scene.

There he lay, a broken pile of tan and dirty white fur, nestled in a sea of his own slobber. Definitely a *he!* His pendulous testicles resembled a pair of radioactive pink grapefruits, and gaudily betrayed his gender. My heart burst with compassion for this poor animal. He was my own precious doggie-gram, sent to me by sacred special delivery from the Great Spirit of Strange Situations.

Now, it was my sacred obligation to doctor the dog.

All through the night I feverishly applied ice packs and good vibes to his busted head. I named him Rex cuz he was so noble . . . no, he was *regal,* and his stoicism at dealing with the suffering succotash that life had dealt him was a wonder to behold. Rex and the sun both rose up as one, miraculously fixed and ready for the new day. I rewarded the wonder dog with a wristwatch for his resurrection. The watch (self-winding) came with a ham bone and a collar.

And so it was that Rex became the official watch and wonder dog of the Hog Farm caravan. To determine the correct time, you had merely to follow the long yellow ropey strands of fresh drool and listen carefully for the ticks and the tocks. Sooner or later you would arrive at Rex and his trusty chronometer.

As a bona fide watchdog with a bona fide function, Rex qualified as crew. This was true, even though he had to be hand-carried on and off the bus to do his (heh, heh!) doggie business.

Late that afternoon we all lit out for New Mexico. It always feels great to be back on the road again. Everyone was real nice to Rex in the beginning because he was a truly funny dog. The fact that Wavy Gravy was in love with this pathetic pooch was also not without humor.

The fun quickly faded with his first fart.

"Pee-yew!"

After an initial barrage of steamy chocolate windbreakers, legions of anti-Rexers sprang up out of nowhere and quickly closed ranks. Even I had to admit they had a legitimate grievance. My incense and air-freshener consumption had skyrocketed in an attempt to appease the more radical and sexist wing of the Hog Farm Ladies Auxiliary.

These nagging biddies demanded that Rex, the watch and wonder dog, enclose those lovely luminous balls of his in a scratchy macramé bag of their own design. All this, so as not to offend their delicate sensibilities.

All this, as we sliced and diced across the highways and biways of the free world in quest of a hippie's dream in the land of southwestern enchantment.

The Southwest furthers. Yippee giddy-up. Whooa!

Our convoy anchors somewhere over Santa Fe and starts to settle in. We score some land in Llano in nearly no time flat. Our own little twelve acres replete with a couple of cracked adobe houses and a well-weathered barn.

Home on the range. Git along you little doggies.

The canine population always seems to expand whenever we park the buses. However, no matter how many hungry hounds showed up for supper they all had to sit and wait patiently for Rex to finish gobbling his fill. Rex had a charming way of arranging his enormous ears in the food dish that grossed out even the other dogs. People would travel great distances to watch the watchdog in action. He even joined a record club, and it is a documented fact that prescription drugs were dispensed to one Rex Romney while I was off traveling in Asia.

When I returned home for my final spinal surgery we successfully smuggled the dog into the Pacific Presbyterian Hospital for a brief visit. I had just been fitted for my Cast of Thousands. Rex's timely visit helped to expedite my discharge from the hospital and subsequent move up to Albion on the Mendocino coast for some heavy healing.

The whole Hog was holed up in a house made of railroad ties. For my afternoon amusement and therapy, kind friends would bring me my basset hound for an afternoon of singing "Summertime." I promised Rex if he practiced regularly and tried real hard he could open at the Copa in the spring in a gold lamé jumpsuit.

Well, spring, sprang, sprung and the telephone ring, rang, rung. It was Jerry Brandt, my old boss from the Electric Circus. He said he was opening a new club in Los Angeles and wondered if I would participate in some way. I said I had this singing dog act. He said we should come on down.

Rex was dashing in his gold lamé jumpsuit. He seemed to enjoy causing all that havoc while crossing Hollywood Boulevard. We slipped into the comparative quiet and safety of the Paradise Ballroom, where the stage manager was my old friend Chip Monck. It was Chip who built the stage at Woodstock. He also invented concert lighting for rock-and-roll. Chip took one look at Rex and said, "Let's fly the dog!"

Mr. Monck was a man of both vision and action. Within moments, a steel wire was hung between the light booth and center stage. Folks down in wardrobe quickly developed the canvas harness that would clip to the wire that would slide old Rex down from the ceiling and onto the stage. It was quite safe. We tested it several times with a sandbag.

Seeing his jumpsuit soaring about like that made Rex act really nervous. Somehow he knew what we were up to, and he just unglued. The poor beast laid down on the floor and reverted to his original pile of gibbering drool. I started scanning the Beverly Hills Yellow Pages in search of a dog psychiatrist who did house calls, but to no avail.

It was cocktail hot dogs that saved the day. Hundreds of tiny little hot dogs that we served him from a silver chafing dish. Nothing's too good for our star.

So, picture this: opening night at the Paradise Ballroom. A gala crowd packs the place. Tuxedos and evening gowns abound. The house lights dim, the excitement builds, and high in the pitch-black ethers of the ceiling there is illuminated one single glowing basset hound. He is jauntily attired in a gold lamé jumpsuit and seems to be floating earthward at great speed. He is also randomly pissing his brains out all over the audience. Saving his final spurts for a United States senator, Rex hits the stage and howls horribly off key.

Well, that's show biz.

It's obviously back to the old time clock for the Rexer. For a few brief moments, however, he was a dashing golden god dispensing liquid karma in his flight. Once at the microphone, however, his rendition of "Summertime" was both rushed and shrill. There was nothing left to do but . . . fade to black. And cue the fire eater.

Fear Itself

For some reason I just love to scare myself. I seek out well-done horror films—you know, the ones that can make you involuntarily leap up in your seat with sudden surprise. I actually enjoy the liftoff. Just lead me to whatever amusement thrill ride that doesn't trash my back. I once rafted in the Stanaslaus rapids with a blind helmsman being directed off the rocks by his wheelchair-bound crewmate. I adore a good close call provided there are no casualties. Yes, you guessed it: I am an adrenaline junkie.

Anything, as long as it's intense, is not only an old Prankster adage, but a code of behavior to evolve by.

It all began innocently enough for me when I was a teenage beatnik. I don't know why I purchased the hundred-dollar roll of tickets for the Coney Island roller coaster. It just seemed like the thing to do at the time. I pondered this as they strapped me into the seat. It wasn't until we began to pull away from the gate and started to climb that the mescaline kicked in.

Whoosh! Over the first drop and then crawling, crawling ever upward, slowly, slowly until the summit's crest and then,

Yaaaaaaaaaaaaaaaaaaaaaaaaaaaaa!

I just loved it.

It was extremely scary for me whenever we stopped. I was afraid someone would net me for having too much fun. In hindsight (this was over thirty years ago) I can see that Coney

Island roller coaster as a cosmic infiltration course for coping with life's little ups and downs on the reality express. Watch out, son, for too much fun. It makes the good lord jealous. Always shoot for just enough, and spread the extra stuff around.

We had a thing going in the old days, when we all lived in a caravan of painted Day-Glo buses, often on the move. If we ever got three flat tires in a row, we would all pull our buses over to the side of the road and have a party. Just break out the wine-in-a-box and boogie till we dropped.

What we were actually up to was consciously having too much fun with our flat tires, and thereby confusing the creator to the point that we stopped having flat tires.

"No more flat tires for those guys," said the Powers That Be. "They're having too much fun."

Evolve, revolve, and dissolve to my current strategy for dealing with the unforeseen.

There is a hundred-year-old Japanese Zen transmission from a woman named Sono. She said, "Every morning, and every evening, and whenever anything happens to you, keep on saying, 'Thanks for everything, I have no complaint whatsoever.' "

Try this the next time you lock your keys in your car.

It helps me to wait for AAA. It also makes me laugh.

Try it yourself, on the occasion of your next flat tire.

Think Hooray for the flat tire, what good fortune! Then stand right up and holler to high heaven, "Thanks for everything, I have no complaint whatsoever!"

For best results you've got to say it like you really mean it. The more difficult the predicament, the funnier the pronouncement.

Even when it's hard.

Broken leg? No problem!

"Thanks for everything, I have no complaint whatsoever."

I could probably pull that off, and have a real good laugh while waiting for the ambulance, provided it didn't hurt too much. When I broke my leg the first time, I went right into shock. It didn't hurt a bit.

It only hurts when I don't laugh. Pain is no fun. Suffering sucks! There is nothing about pain that intrigues me. Even growing pains!

Question: If growing is painful, could shrinking induce pleasure?

Remember the incredible shrinking man. He just got smaller and smaller until he vanished in thin air. What a way to go.

"Thanks for everything. I have no complaint whatsoever."

Poof.

I Love Paris in the Hospital

"It only hurts when you don't laugh. Laughter is like the valve on the pressure cooker of life. You either laugh at stuff or you end up with your beans or your brains on the ceiling. If you don't have a sense of humor, it just isn't funny anymore." I forget who said that stuff, but I'll testify to its authenticity.

I remember how it was for me after my third spinal surgery. I was gnashing my teeth from one day to the next, bitter, battered, and bored. The pain was both deep and dull. It seemed to coat my every action. My sense of humor was totally *smushed*. . . . Then these docs from the Oakland Children's Hospital fell by our house. They had read something about me in the local paper and wondered if I could stop by the hospital from time to time and cheer up the kids.

Something within me said, "Sure, I'll give it a shot." At this point I was bouncing on the bottom, and had nothing to lose.

The following day I decided to go for it. On the way out the front door somebody handed me a red rubber nose. The rest is history.

Henry Ford once said, "History is bunk." I like Kurt Vonnegut's definition: "History is a list of surprises."

That day at the hospital was a little shaky because it was my first time and I was kinda feeling my way around. Without the clown nose I could have struck out completely. With the nose I was able to move outside of my bummer and make little kids laugh, which was something they really needed to do. It's real scary to find yourself in strange surroundings without your parents, and in pain. I thought I had troubles till I eyeballed some of these kids.

Eash day I'd go back and get a little bit better as this clown thing I had fallen into, and each night I'd come home feeling a whole lot better about my own situation. I got so I could go hours at a time focused on some kid. My own pain would all but disappear.

It was never me putting on a show for the children or anything like that. Mainly it involved just hanging out with each individual kid, and feeling around for what was most appropriate. Reading a story, swapping jokes and riddles. Bubbles were, and are, the ultimate ice-breaker.

The first time I showed up in full clown makeup this little six-year-old just about had a conniption fit. Over the years I discovered about 15 percent of all kids are terrified of clowns. The other 85 percent just eat 'em up. I never figured out why that is. Maybe they were just trapped in this antiseptic nightmare of glass and chrome when this giant bozo leaped up and started honking his big red nose in their face. I began to put my makeup on at the hospital, in front of the youngest children. It sort of de-monsterfied the clown and made the kids feel safe.

One day I had to go to a political rally at the Peoples Park and didn't have time to take my makeup off. I just dashed over there and found that the police didn't want to hit me any more. Why? *Clowns are safe!*

My first true test came after about a year of clowning around the wards. I had the giant shoes this old clown had passed on to me when he retired. He heard about my trip and wanted his feet to go on walking. The shoes were two-toned wingtips made for Ringling Brothers in the forties.

Well sir, I stomped right smack into the middle of this young child's death. I had no idea what was going on. It was kind of like stepping into a vacuum, or the Bermuda triangle, with nurses running around pulling drapes and closing doors; and doctors desperately pretending everything was normal. It was some kind of mechanical drill they were trapped in. Everyone was extremely relieved to see my bubbles come bursting through their false and impersonal charade. I felt right away I had entered a very privileged space that was as holy as the many births I had been fortunate enough to witness, yet these trained professionals did all they could to deny the existence of death and pretend it just wasn't happening. I felt something was really out of whack.

In the library I discovered the writing of Elisabeth Kübler-Ross and her pioneering book, *On Death and Dying*. I absorbed everything she wrote and tuned into the American hospice movement, then still in its infancy. I even went to several lectures by Dr. Charles Garfield and learned of the Shanti Project, which uses trained laypeople to assist folks in dying at home. I didn't know if a death would ever come up for me again with these kids, but if it did I wanted to be ready.

One day the head nurse had me summoned to the control-center telephone. On the other end was Paris. In her eleven years of life on the planet, Paris had received almost one hundred operations for cancer. She had one leg and played shortstop for the little league. Paris was a bona fide superstar who would beat down grounders with her wooden leg. She said she had been watching me for over a year. She also said she was coming back into the hospital for an operation to remove a cancer near her heart and how would I like to be her clown companion? I answered in the affirmative and we met formally when she checked into the hospital the following day.

Forget Sinead O'Connor or that bald and foxy sweetie from *Star Trek*. Paris's skull was a symphony of skin over bone so flawless and smooth it took my breath away. This may sound a tad off the deep and kinky end, but I assure you it was nothing like that. She was quite simply a beautiful child. Her eyes were extremely alert as she scanned my clowntinance; twin lasers checking me out. I felt her eyes travel . . . up, down, and sideways till they landed on my instrument case.

"Whatcha got in there?" she wondered.

"It's a one-string instrument from India called an *iktar. Ek,* in Hindu, means one. I guess *tar* could mean string." (I tell people, "Many strings . . . never in tune. One string . . . sometimes I get lucky.") I picked up the iktar and started plunking away. "Row, row, row your boat," I sang. "Gently down the stream. I fooled you! I fooled you! Cuz I'm a submarine!" Paris howled with laughter. "What's so funny?" I asked her.

"You are!" she answered and I knew I had arrived. I felt invincible and immediately broke into "The Farmer in the Dell." When I got to the part about the cheese, Paris began to weep and I instinctively ate her tears. (I mean I wiped her tears from her face with my finger, which I then stuck in my mouth.) It was a first for both of us. We were oblivious to her mother's horror over my unsanitary antics.

By the time her surgery date was upon us, Paris and I were a fully bonded unit. The moment she was thirsty I handed her water. I just *knew* whenever she wanted something. I had never been this close to another human being and when it came time for Paris to go under the knife I became extremely involved in trying to cover all the bases.

I went so far as to phone every radio station in the Bay Area. I badgered program directors and disk jockeys alike. My plan was to make as many people as possible conscious of Paris and her upcoming surgery, so that they would beam healing energy in her direction. It was amazing how many stations complied. The surgeon stated after the successful operation that he felt like a marionette with ''invisible strings'' aiding him in his work.

Her recovery was swift and remarkable, but not for Paris Duchamp. She taught me everything I know about courage without ever saying a word.

Within a month she was dirt-biking in Oregon.

Six months later Paris died peacefully in her bed while her mother shopped for groceries.

We never got to say good-bye. We didn't need to. Every time it gets really hard for me in this life and I have to reach beyond myself, Paris slips into my heart and we do it together. Sometimes with laughter, but always with joy, which is simply the grease of God.

Sacred Places

I recently attended a presentation of slides shown to promote a picture book of the world's sacred places. Stonehenge, Glastonbury, the Grand Canyon, the Ganges, the pyramids, et cetera. I had visited more than a few of these spiritual hot spots in my lifetime, and so I was able to float my own trip on to the images being offered. I imagined that was me bathing with the sadus in the Ganges, or cooling it in the kiva with the Hopi, or climbing with my sherpa up the slippery face of K2.

The tiny auditorium was just dark enough for me to hover somewhere between half-divine daydream and half-astral projection.

Then the other half kicked in. I started to get higher and higher. Now, I'm dining with druids at Stonehenge, munching with Merlin in the Glastonbury Tor, noshing with Noah after he landed the ark in the Atlas Mountains of Turkey, where he worshipped the very first rainbow. I remember traveling with the Hog Farm through those mountains. We were in a big hurry because it was so cold. Our sleeping bags were freezing to the inside walls of the bus. One night the gas froze in the lines while we were driving the bus. A Turkish truck driver came to our aid by placing a pile of wood under the bus and setting it on fire.

"When the lines thaw, you drive like hell," he suggested.

We were doing just that when we were forced off the road

by a big-time blizzard. In the morning we found ourselves on the outskirts of a tiny Kurdish village that sat on the side of Mount Ararat. It was here, perhaps, that Noah ran the ark aground. A Russian archaeological exhibition had recently photographed fossilized fragments of . . .

"Oh, sir!" said the janitor, lightly shaking my shoulder. "Wake up, please. Everybody's gone home."

The lights are on. The slide show is over. The hall is nearly empty.

"You really got out there didn't you, sir? Say, aren't you Wavy Gravy?"

I nodded groggily to the tie-dyed custodian and shook the snows of Asia Minor out of my ears.

"No, don't get up. Take your time. Just remember to lock up when you leave. Boy, I'll bet you've been to some pretty far-out places in your lifetime. What if you had to pick just one?"

That question hung over my head long after that hippie was history. Then it submerged itself in the waters of my brain, where it bubbled and wubbled around for a while, before revealing the answer:

Atlanta!

Atlanta?

Yes, absolutely. I don't know why it should come as such a shock. I remember being utterly blown away at the time. In fact, I thought I had been dosed. It happened in the spring of '88. I had just finished presenting a hands-on seminar on humor to the staff of the New Leaf New Age book distributors. That company is run by my good friends Halim and Natalie. It was they who first took me to visit the memorial built to honor Dr. Martin Luther King, Jr.

The King Memorial is also a national monument. It is located in downtown Atlanta, just down the street from the

Ebenezer Baptist Church. There is a sepulcher where Dr. King is buried, a reflecting pool, an eternal flame, a meditation chapel, and a modest museum. All built out of the same pale white marble.

When we arrived, all the staff was either off duty or having a meeting. A stiff wind had blown out the eternal flame and scattered gladioli all over the sepulcher.

The incredible power of the place suddenly surrounded me like a sheath of liquid crystal, as we bent to pick up the flowers and re-eternalize the eternal flame.

"Eternity now," I uttered, sitting down abruptly on the edge of the reflecting pool. Just then the waters around me exploded with rainbows. The pool expanded and contracted and time turned sideways. The reflecting pool was now enormous, running all the way from the Washington Monument to the Lincoln Memorial. People and buses were everywhere, hundreds of thousands of people, a symphony of black and beige and brown. The heat of the day is oppressive and folks are availing themselves of the waters of the pool to cool off. They were purposefully wetting their bandannas and soaking their hot and tired feet.

This was at the culmination of the great March for Civil Rights in Washington, D.C.

I had become separated from my friends in the Living Theater. They had chartered the bus that brought me down from New York City. There were thousands of buses in Washington that day. Buses from all over America.

I started edging my way toward the Lincoln Memorial where a stage had been erected to accommodate the many speakers scheduled to address the crowd. I had just wiggled my way to the street when I ran smack into Peter, Paul, and Mary on their way up to that very stage. They swept me into their entourage, and the next time I blinked I was backstage with Bob

Dylan and Joan Baez. We were standing just a few feet from Dr. King when he launched into his famous "I Have a Dream" speech.

I remember whispering in Dylan's ear, "I hope he's over quick. Mahalia Jackson's on next."

Then the air turned to liquid crystal filled with rainbows, and I didn't care if he never stopped speaking.

Then on came Mahalia with her hot ticket to heaven.

That's when I saw it.

At the white marble foot of the statue of Abraham Lincoln lay a half-eaten piece of southern fried chicken.

"Look at that!" I hollered, to everybody in particular. "Now, see the grease on his thumb and his forefinger. Look at the crumbs and shortening glistening in his marble beard."

"Eternity Now."

And somehow I'm back in Atlanta. Natalie has gathered up all the fallen gladioli. She is now wading across the reflecting pool to replace them in the empty marble vase at the base of Dr. King's tomb. Halim is busily engaged in washing my feet in the pool with his Seva T-shirt.

"Don't get paranoid," he suggested. "They're used to weird behavior around here."

Hunter Thompson once said, "When the going gets tough the weird turn pro."

I think of Martin Luther King, Jr., as an authentic American saint and every molecule of this monument as a sacred testimony to that assessment. Recent rumors suggest he had a weakness for women other than his wife. If that is so, it makes his life and deeds all the more accessible for the likes of me.

Eternity Now!

And I click my heels again and I'm safely back in Berkeley.

What's in a Name?

My son was born in the back of our bus, parked at a Tomahawk truckstop just outside Boulder, Colorado. We named him Howdy Do-good Tomahawk Truckstop Gravy. We called him Howdy, Howdy Do-good, or Howdy Do-good Gravy, depending on our mood. The Tomahawk Truckstop was both understood and silent. When Howdy was thirteen years old he entered my room and firmly announced, "I'm too old to be Howdy."

Who was I to argue? I've been through more names than most kids have gone through sneakers. "Wavy Gravy" fell out of the sky at the Texas Pop Festival with the blessing of blues great B. B. King, and was formally adopted at Cal State in Alhambra, California, in the fall of '69.

I was teaching improvisation and theater games to a new group of neurologically disabled children and I began the class with the following spiel: "Hi, kids. My name is Wavy Gravy . . ." After we had finished the class, the professors, who had been observing my efforts through one-way glass, came running into the room and said, "Keep that name, you saved a week's orientation!"

I've been Wavy Gravy for over twenty years now, and you won't believe the amount of orientation I've saved.

My name is a great door-opener, but a problem on the phone. Somehow a person actually named Wavy Gravy is just too much for a telephone operator to cope with. They simply snarl and hang up.

Gravy, first initial W., is all they can deal with. So be it.

My wife Bonnie Jean (code name: Country Pie) became Jahanara at the bequest of her Sufi teacher at least ten years ago. Although never in Jamaica, we call her Jah for short. When our son requested a name change, we two didn't have a leg to stand on.

"Well, what do you want to call yourself," I asked.

"Jordan Beecher Romney," came his swift reply.

I knew Marcellus Jordan was a handsome child of color and his closest friend; Beecher was Jah's maiden name; and Romney was part of my given family name.

What's the rest, you wonder.

Well it's Hugh Nanton Romney. How do you like them apples? Hardly a Wavy Gravy in the basket. I still use it as an a.k.a. and keep it on my driver's license in case I have to disappear . . .

"Wavy Gravy? Never heard of him. Excuse me, I have to call my broker."

A clever ploy that hasn't worked in fifteen years. The police know almost all my names by heart.

In point of fact, when I went downtown to bail out Jordan Beecher Romney when he was busted with his teenage cronies from "Creating Our Future" for occupying the Japanese Trade Center in protest of their decimation of the Malaysian rainforest, I was careful to wear my straightest clothes and flourish my Hugh Romney driver's license for the desk sergeant.

He took one brief look and had two patrolmen escort me to the real jail, while the kids were detained in the day room.

"Scram, Gravy ain't Wavy," and "You're never off the bus," the officers babbled through the bars.

What's in a name, you might ask. Well, you can keep your precious Moon Units and your splendid Sunday Peaches, and even stick with Flying Rainbow Snail. Hugh Romney, however, was finally released from custody with the kids he came to rescue.

At age fourteen, Howdy Do-good Tomahawk Truckstop Gravy changed his name in court to Jordan Beecher Romney. He is now nineteen years old, still Jordan, and still very much at large.

Trungpa

I have a blank spot in my brain that fades in and out for about six years of my life. These great gaps of memory fall all the way from my last spinal surgery until my first (and only) near-death experience, and subsequent resurrection. Many amazing things transpired during that time of which I have little or no recollection.

Take the incident of one Chogyam Trungpa Rinpoche. He was one of the anointed lamas of Tibet. It was Chogyam Trungpa who brought the sacred teachings of the backroom buddhas to the free world, and was paralyzed on one side of his face due to a collision with a Scotch practical joke shop while driving into the sunset with another man's wife.

Given that my rememberer was out of commission for the aforementioned incident, I will pass the job of recollection over to my good friend Dr. Lawrence Brilliant. Larry remembers bringing me to Berkeley in 1972 to hear Trungpa's first public talk. It was shortly after my final fusion, so I was encased in that plaster body cast I mentioned earlier.

The Dharmadhatu storm troopers at the door took exception to my choice of political buttons, Chairman Mao and the Dalai Lama. The former left and facing right and the latter right and facing left. (I remember none of this.) Larry tells me that I said, "It's a pair o' Dux."

And then I laid down, front row center, resembling an

all-too-animated ottoman at the foot of the absent Trungpa's throne. (I actually remember the throne and the flowers and the flagon of Drambuie on the side.)

Trungpa was late, very late. The crowd was restless but reverent with one skinny exception. Me.

I was busy inflating Larry's balloon stash as fast as I could blow, and then bouncing them out into the assemblage. (This is an old Hog Farm ploy, used to loosen up almost any situation.) Somehow I had affixed a burning candle to my plaster middle. (This was understandable, having recently emerged from several months' incarnation as a coffee table.)

Trungpa swept into the hall, pausing only to extinguish my candle with the pop of an errant balloon. His ascension to the throne was so awkward I could only ascertain that this lama was a little loaded. A loaded lama in a three-piece suit smoking a Marlboro and lecturing on impermanence between dainty belts of honeyed scotch. It was more than I could bear.

"What about Bangladesh?" I bleated.

Bangladesh was the buzzword of the moment for that spot of greatest suffering on the planet. I knew I was a little out of line but this extremely high lama was suggesting we should all stop trying to feed the hungry and stop the war, and

Meditate.

Meditate . . . meditate, meditate, and keep on meditating, until you are enlightened, for Christ's sake.

"What about Bangladesh?" I repeated from the floor in what Dr. Larry later suggested was the first public heckle of a high Tibetan lama.

He neatly worked me into his act, though, saying something like, "You cannot do anything for the suffering of the world unless you are first enlightened . . . and then you gotta work till everyone else is enlightened . . ."

To which I replied, "What about the starving people in Bangladesh?"

To which he replied, "You simply do not understand! You cannot help them. Karma is karma. The starving people of Bangladesh are beyond your food."

This guy was making his monologue a dialogue. Larry suggested we were engaged in a contemporary rendition of the eternal debate between service and compassion. All I know is he started passing me his cigarettes and booze while we beat the breeze on these heavy issues. I was obviously enjoying this ancient argument, especially after the Drambuie kicked in. Then I gave up.

"Okay, I will work ceaselessly for enlightenment. But while I am doing that I will help feed the people of Bangladesh."

Trungpa laughed out loud. It was just like the ballet with the buttons at the door. Another pair o' Dux.

As the lama went to make his exit I heard an admirer ask him, "Do you know *who that man is?*" He was looking at me.

He paused in parting, turned and said, *"That* man is self-explanatory."

Even I remember that.

Santa

Here is a shot of me in one of my many Santa Claus incarnations. Mr. Claus entered my adult life as a vision that had nothing to do with sugar plums—or even Christmas, for that matter.

The year was 1980 when a phalanx of Santas came cascading across my frontal lobe. That's right, a phalanx of Santa Clauses. What a weapon in the arsenal of civil disobedience. In my mind's eye I saw these Clauses in action at the Lawrence Livermore Weapons Laboratory. Then, on the six o'clock news of my imagination, I watched the police and Santas try to mix it up. It was always a standoff, cuz no cop would dare take on a Santa on color TV.

Santa Claus was safe.

I scored my first Santa suit at a Pay 'n' Save on the outskirts of Oakland. I stuck it in the closet and waited for the rest of the phalanx to materialize. It was well into summer when I finally realized that I was *it*. John Q. Phalanx. That's me. An army of one. All dressed up and no place to go.

Enter the Abalone Alliance. The alliance was made up of hundreds of small affinity groups scattered throughout California. Mine was called the Mutant Sponges. We were all pledged to commit acts of non-violent civil disobedience to prevent the start-up of the Diablo Canyon Nuclear Power Plant just outside San Luis Obispo on the Hogosa earthquake fault. Just the cause for Mr. Claus.

I decided to conceal my identity as Santa until the ultimate moment of arrest. I would wear my costume hidden under my U.S. Navy bright green catapult jumpsuit with lots of Velcro instead of zippers—specially designed for aircraft carrier crews. I could turn into Santa in a second. Just hit the Velcro and jingle my bells.

And it did come to pass that me and the Mutant Sponges scaled the barbed-wire fence that surrounded the reactor in one of the early waves. Then we all linked arms and marched along the narrow asphalt road that led to Diablo proper.

Enter the phalanx of fuzz.

As soon as we saw them we sat down in the road and started singing, "We shall not, we shall not be moved. We shall not . . ."

These police had other ideas. Just as their captain read us the order to disperse I noticed a police film crew scurrying into position. They were going to be filming our arrest. They were in the process of making a training aid film to teach other police the correct way of dealing with people like us. I couldn't believe my good fortune! I looked my arresting officers straight in the eye as they reached out to cuff and catalogue me. Then I hit the Velcro and turned into jolly old St. Nick.

"Don't mess with me, or you'll get nothing in your socks," I shouted. "I have militant elves that will go for your kneecaps."

These cops bit their lips to keep from laughing and went on about their jobs. They pretended not to notice my outrageous attire. It wasn't until later, when I got to jail, that I overheard a fellow inmate reenacting his bust. He quoted the police: "Don't mess with us," they said. "We busted Santa Claus."

That made me feel a lot better.

Inside, they took away my beard. No problem, I made another one out of paper. Santa's been to jail before. I'm talking big-time, way back when in Asia Minor. They don't call him *Saint* Nicholas for nothing. I'm sure he suffered in that serious slammer. We've come a long way, penally, in the last thousand years.

They locked up all the men arrested at Diablo Canyon in the Questa College gymnasium. We then proceeded to turn the college into the University of the Cosmos. There were classes in Gandhian theory and the nonviolent training of trainers. We had juggling classes, yoga classes, basketball, and in the evening I would slip on my paper whiskers and emcee the talent show. We always kicked it off with a couple choruses of "Jingle Bells" or "Santa Claus Is Coming to Town." (This was in the middle of August, mind you. If I did it in December it wouldn't be nearly as weird.) At this point I would waddle up to the invisible microphone in my Santa stuff and holler, "Yes, you too can be sucked up in the tornado of talent." And whoever had signed up would step up and let'er rip.

When the police busted Jackson Browne I persuaded the captain to smuggle in a guitar. We had the hottest ticket in California! The guards began to smuggle in their wives to catch our show.

This was some amazing kinda jail that can only exist when you get a couple thousand people in one place, all ready to take a fall for what they believe in.

The real jails of America are way too crowded to accommodate such antisocial behavior, so they have to put us in these pretend jails. Like field houses, circus tents, and, in this case, the Questa College gymnasium. There, they surround us with police and won't let us go home until they say so, or until our lawyers get us cut loose. They call this time punishment, and it is so much fun that a lot of us refuse to leave unless we can all leave together. This is called jail-bail solidarity. Gandhi and Dr.

King were deep into this. If more of us were into it in the sixties we could have tried to shut down Vietnam a little sooner.

No, we didn't shut down the Diablo reactor, but God knows we tried. We did prove it was unsafe when we started the action. (Upon reviewing the blueprints, the Nuclear Regulatory Commission found that some sections were put together backwards.) And you notice those suckers aren't sprouting up like mushrooms anymore.

In court I pleaded insanity. I told the judge it was insane to build a nuclear reactor on an earthquake fault. He said I had a point there, and sent me back to the gym to finish my time.

After two weeks they had to toss me out. The guards tried to work out a special deal where I would slip back in each evening and emcee the tornado of talent, but the regulations clearly stated blah, blah, blah.

Once on the outside, one of the more radicalized prison guards suggested I try my hand at improving communications. Relatives and friends of the detainees of Hotel Diablo were forced to yell messages to their loved ones from across the street into the exercise yard with its necklace of barbed wire. It took me just under three hours to panhandle enough cash to purchase a Three Mile Loud Hailer, complete with microphone, batteries, and a jack for a tape deck.

This was the birth of my Fun Company, which I ran as Santa out of the back of this imaginary sled. Friends would tell Santa (that's me, stripped down to hat, beard, and bright red bikini panties) the name of the person they wanted to page and Santa would crank up the bullhorn and make the announcement—"Joe Blow, Joe Blow . . . White Courtesy Telephone Please."

And when Joe would show, I'd relinquish the mike and folks would be able to communicate with each other. From nine in the morning until just after dark the airwaves would abound with love and goodwill. We set up a little welcome center in the back of the sled where we dispensed fruit juice, vitamins, beer, and chi to the unincarcerated. I'm sure St. Nicholas woulda dug it. Even though it wasn't exactly Asia Minor and this Santa ain't no saint. You gotta suffer to be a saint.

I got to live out my fantasy as a phalanx one more time at the Lawrence Livermore Labs, then again on the tracks of the Concord Naval Weapons Station. The very same tracks that claimed the legs of Brian Wilson the year before.

I had the somewhat dubious honor of being arrested on the exact spot where that train refused to stop. But it wasn't the train or the tracks that must bare that awful blame for Brian's legs, but the engineer who only followed orders, the commander who gave them, and this country who could condone such a train-wreck of the heart.

As the cop closed his handcuffs on the wrists of Mr. Claus, a photographer from Associated Press froze us forever in the national press. It was a minor bust and I was out in plenty of time to revisit the tracks that Christmas morning.

The occasion was the presentation to Brian Wilson of his brand-new artificial legs by Santa Claus. This was the Wavy Gravy perk of a lifetime. I even had my own elf, who doubled as a rigger for the prosthesis. This was a major media event for our side. I did my ho, ho, ho for the television cameras and left the installation to the elf.

Off with the old, but before the new could go on we all cringed with horror at the sight of his hideous stumps. Then Brian forever blew our hearts and minds, as he showed us and the press how he changed those stumps into balding little puppets for the kids. He de-horrified the horror and helped to heal us all. Forget the miracle of water into wine. This man maintains his sense of humor in the very heart of hell.

I love to go to jail with Brian. The last time out, I was dressed as the Easter bunny. I was carrying my big sign that says MUTANT BUNNIES FOR PEACE—SAVE THE HUMANS. Whenever I wear my bunny suit I always sport a tiny keychain with this little plastic human foot attached for luck.

"Is that one of mine?" inquired Brian as he adjusted his St. Louis Cardinals cap to accommodate the halo. I knew at that moment there was hope for us all in the real alchemy of turning our terror into fun.

God bless Saint Brian Wilson.

God bless us every one.

Winnarainbow

"Hi Camp."

"Rainbow Junction."

"Camp Runn-a-mucca."

"Winnarainbow!" said Surya Singer and we knew we had it.

It was the perfect name for our kids' camp. We had been brainstorming for over a week when it burst full-blown like a lightbulb blazing over my partner's Afro. Camp Winnarainbow was born over fifteen years ago in the Mendocino Woodlands of northern California. We started out doing improvisational daycare for an already existing camp for Sufi adults. It seemed to me that parents should not be penalized spiritually because they had children. So we took them on, with a lot of help from our friends: artists, dancers, mimes. Surya was a genius theatrical director and ex big-time yogi who was re-tooling as a slack rope walker and juggler. I was the dean of improvisation and intuition. The chemistry between us was exceptional.

Surya's wife Sarada picked up the loose ends as we swiftly segued our scene into an overnight kids' camp. We found that parents got in the way of any real advancement for themselves or their children. They needed the time to focus on their meditations and spiritual practices while the kids needed the space to work out their inner dependence and their juggling.

Overnight camp was an overnight sensation. We began to

draw from the New Age spiritual community and the rock-and-roll cabals of the Bay Area. Sessions were short and sweet, culminating with the camp play, which Surya and I would dream up in a couple of golden afternoons. The play would feature all the skills taught at Winnarainbow strung together with a bare-bones plot that he and I would narrate and whip into shape in a few days. We began to tour our ten-day wonder camp to locations in New Mexico and New York. Early extravaganzas included tales of Krishna, Monkey, and St. Francis, followed by one about 20/20 vision, which took place in the year 2020 in an old clown's home. The play featured a team of aliens who landed in a flying saucer searching for the gift of laughter.

Then came the History of the Circus, Parts 1 and 2. We began with cave people juggling rocks and Christians walking a tightrope over a pit of lions. We also touched on the jesters and jugglers of the Middle Ages, the commedia dell'arte of Italy, and the harlequins of the French court.

In Part 2 we moved from equestrian exhibitions in England to the New World. We saw Dan Rice, an early American clown who served as the model for Uncle Sam, teach Abraham Lincoln how to juggle. Into each production were woven the songs of the summer, set in elaborate production numbers involving the whole camp.

When the Hog Farm purchased the Black Oak Ranch we moved out of the quaint but congested cabins of the Mendocino woodlands and into a circle of teepees five miles north of Laytonville. That was the year we would lose my good friend and partner Surya Singer to the Christian community. He has been resurrected as "Righteous" Ron Singer, teacher of high school English and juggler for Jesus. He and his wife Sarada left a great void we have long struggled to fill.

Jahanara has taken over the linear structure from Sarada

and is now co-director of Winnarainbow. She and her assistants, Michele and Lois, have put our whole scene on computer. We now run Camp Winnarainbow for six weeks each summer for children, and one week for adults. Experimental adult camp is just like kids' camp except you can stay up, not brush your teeth, and procreate.

A typical day at Winnarainbow begins at eight o'clock with the blowing of a conch shell and a hearty, "Lets go, Coco!" Kids stagger sporadically out of their respective tepees in the general direction of the camp kitchen for hot chocolate, and the bathrooms for flushing and brushing. This is followed by final wake-up and breakfast. Then comes teepee cleanup and then, the gathering in the outdoor theater for the morning reading. I read from the *Tao Te Ching,* the *Almanac* (birthdays, historical events, and astrological occurrences), and *Everything I Need to Know I Learned in Kindergarten.* Vocalizations and singing take up another fifteen minutes. By then their breakfast is well digested and we can begin our morning warm-ups. The warm-ups help us avoid camper injury, as does our compulsory falling class, which every kid must pass before moving on to study circus skills.

At the end of each morning's exercises, we re-gather in the theater and discover what is being offered in the two class periods that proceed showtime, when we share what we learned with the rest of the camp. A typical list of presentations would feature juggling, tightrope, trapeze, stilt-walking, unicycle riding, clowning, acting, improvisation, dance (modern, jazz, African, belly, can-can, tap, hip-hop, street, et cetera), martial arts, nature walks, art class, music (singing, drumming, guitar, songwriting), gymnastics, mime, and survival skills. Swimming lessons are given in the morning to those campers who have not passed their basic swim test.

All children must learn to swim at Camp Winnarainbow.

That may sound a tad strong. Are we Winnafascists? You betcha—but only to avoid serious accidents and life-threatening injury. We want to make Camp Winnarainbow the safest place on earth, so kids who can't already swim must attend those classes. All swimming prowess is acknowledged and rewarded but none more so than learning to swim from the shoreline to the raft and back again. (The raft is named George.)

Lake Veronica is three acres of water on the Hog Farm land picturesquely penetrated by a 350-foot water slide. (But I precede myself.)

After all the classes are announced, the kids go off with the presenter of their choice. After an hour, the sound of a conch announces it's time to move on to the second and final class of the morning. Then we meet in the theater and share what we learned. This is both boring and vital, especially early on, because we buzz, "if you can see it, you can be it!" In other words, when one sweet and clumsy, run-of-the-mill normal nerd like me can learn to juggle three balls, ride a unicycle, or qualify on high stilts, that means there's hope for us all.

Everybody has a good shot at learning to do everything we teach at camp. For the first three days we ask the kids to try everything at least once. Then they are free to follow their bliss through the summer. It's a chance for them to push the corners of their evolving envelopes with safety and supervision. We in no way attempt to turn out legions of actors or circus stars; instead, we encourage universal human beings with an equal mastery of timing, balance, and compassion, coupled with an uncanny ability to duck with a sense of humor.

Once this was just a definition and a dream. Today it is actualized in so many amazing kids who started out as seven-year-olds attending camp for a few short weeks and returning year after year. They do their growing right along with the rest of us and pass from camper (up to age fourteen) on to the teen or teaching staff. Former campers make our finest counselors.

Our first wave of Winnarainbozos are well underway. They are attending colleges and universities, entering the marketplace, or just traveling about. Whatever they are up to, I figure they have a jump-start on the rest of the herd, because they have developed a piece of their brain that is all but ignored in traditional schooling, a piece so necessary in dealing with the daily slings and arrows of life. I call it "Survival in the twenty-first century, or how to duck with a sense of humor." Add a generous dollop of compassion and understanding and there may be hope for us all.

After showtime we wash our hands and eat lunch. Meals are served out of a beautiful kitchen set in the forest and designed by my dad. We eat on wooden picnic tables. Almost all the produce is organically grown on Black Oak Ranch, which is the historic name for the Hog Farm country land.

In our early years, Winnarainbow rented a cluster of tiny cabins with a combination mess hall/rec hall in the Mendocino redwoods. After-dark discipline was difficult, as each cabin held about four kids. We would dart about, shushing the children like Keystone Kamper kontrol. Eventually, we would drop in our tracks or the kids would grow bored and fall asleep.

Swimming was performed at a nearby nude beach. We would show up at this idyllic, out of the way, sun and swim spot, which was usually crowded on the hot days. Not only did our kids get a quick anatomy lesson, they could clear the beach of everybody but us in less than half an hour. It was a great gift from God that we survived those early years without serious injury. Now we have five lifeguards at our own lake, and we are insured up to the eyeballs.

After we moved, Jahanara got everyone at camp to write up risk-management reports on their field of expertise. The figures were fed into the camp computer and mailed to the

American Camping Association for accreditation, which we received, much to the amazement of almost everyone except Jah.

I wrote my report on wrist-rocketry, or, in the vernacular, "slingshots." I have safely operated a slingshot range at Camp Winnarainbow for fifteen years. As in the best of activities, the rules revealed themselves over time and circumstance. I get the kids to form an orderly line about thirty feet from the target. *No cuts!* You may leave the line safely only if you have secured the permission of the persons to the front and rear of your place in line. Only when you are third from the front can you pick up an unloaded wrist rocket and practice your pull and release. When it is your turn to shoot you may place a rock in the leather tongue, toe the line, and shoot at one of three inflated balloons, which constitute the targets. You are awarded three rocks per turn. Each hit counts as one point and earns an additional rock. A pop is three points and another rock. If you call a particular balloon and pop it, you get five points, and if you hit it you get three points. If you hit or pop a balloon other than the one you called, you receive nothing. Once you get nine points you graduate from singles. The next day you advance to doubles (twice the distance) and start on a fresh nine points.

Each time you advance distances, you are acknowledged in the evening circle and get to come into my campsite and pick a suitable reward from my prize stash, or from the crystal garden. You would be amazed, as I was, at how many children prefer a crystal to a water pistol.

There is more than one way to cop a crystal at Camp Winnarainbow. You can be gloriously good and receive a stroke at dinner circle (six strokes equals one crystal). Or you can be bad and get a strike. Three strikes and you're out. Seldom, almost never, is a child sent home. Hitting is a major no-no, and is an automatic three strikes and a phone call to the parents. This is a brand-new policy designed to make camp safe for everyone. It entails a lot of hard work in quest of the perfect world in microcosm. That's what we're really after in those eight short summer weeks—the perfect world.

Afternoons at camp are generally spent at the lake swimming and enjoying that new waterslide we got from Marine World/Africa U.S.A. This is not compulsory. Afternoons are basically free time. My wife was severely traumatized at her childhood camp by being forced to write a letter home each day. At Winnarainbow no one writes home unless they really want to, which is actually, quite often.

Some kids take a supervised hike downstream to visit the mud baths. Others are involved in skill practice, rehearsal, or just lazing about the teepee circle. We live and sleep in a circle of beautiful fireproof canvas teepees sewed by Intents, the teepee and awning business run by Dorgie Chase. She and Sindi Petti have also developed our costume stash over the years until it has achieved its current extensive status. Young female campers achieve near nirvana as they are able to change clothes all summer long.

The teepee circle is an old idea that still functions exquisitely for us in the present day. Each unit contains a counselor, junior counselor or teen staffer, and seven campers. All their gear folds up against the wall during the day and rolls out at night for sleeping. Each teepee door opens out into the firepit at the center of the circle. Unlike those golden days we spent dashing from cabin to cabin at the Woodlands, our nighty-nite scene is a wonder to behold!

But wait, we haven't even had dinner yet. In the late afternoon, pick-up skills and crafts are offered along with some form of sport. Softball, volleyball, Ultimate Frisbee. . . . Then a conch is blown to announce the evening circle, which is a panoply of songs, awards, and announcements. Each day a different teepee gets to eat first, and then they wash the dishes. This happens only twice a session, unless you are working off some strikes. Before dinner we offer graces, which are multidenominational and spoken at random by both campers and staff.

After dinner there is a short period of free time, followed by the evening program. This can be a talent show, fire circle, dance, film, or adventure night. At the end of the evening program I holler, "Brush 'em if you got 'em!" This evokes the toothbrush dance. Then the weary campers retire to their teepees to talk over the day's events or share a story or a song—until lights out is sounded and they sleep. . . . And then another day.

What began as creative daycare for a handful of Sufi children in the seventies has entered the nineties as a multidenominational nonprofit wonderland. Our staff of fifty accommodates close to three hundred kids in the course of a summer. Seventy percent of the parents can well afford our righteously reasonable rates. Fifteen percent attend on partial scholarship. Our full-scholarship campers are selected by Jah, in close collaboration with state and city agencies, to include the homeless, battered, sexually abused, refugees, and indigenous children who help to make up our very real rainbow.

As the artistic and creative director, it is my job to keep experimenting with new concepts, and reshuffling the working wonder so the winds of change can blow through old doorways and keep our living truth alive. The first play on the new land was *Coyote Capers,* which let us share in the laughter, as well as the tears, of native people.

The rainbow stage was created for *The Golden Key* by George McDonald. *Peace Kids* was my adaptation of the international triumph *Peace Child.* Its demanding script was a near disaster in our limited time frame. What was amazing about *Peace Kids* was that special talk I held for all the teens and any other kids who promised to conduct themselves as young adults while we discussed the threat of nuclear annihilation of the planet. Each person in that circle got to speak their true heart song. I would encourage world leaders to listen to the dreams and fears of these children.

Lately, we have moved our focus to the environment, with equally powerful results. Our *All Species Congress* was drawn from the book *Thinking Like a Mountain*. One of its authors, John Seed, of the Australian Rainforest Coalition, came to camp and led us through a session of evolutionary remembering. We began with the Big Bang and evolved from the basic elements, and through primordial soup to the one-celled life form. From there we journeyed into the age of amphibians, dinosaurs, apes, and so on until we reached the present time.

Each year we seem to get a better bead on who and where we are and the incredible interconnectedness of all living things. We do a fire circle, where each teepee speaks for an endangered species and creates masks to represent their choice. It is a deep and moving ceremony.

Our end-of-session plays have evolved into revues, like "All's Fair in Love and Peace." The camping area is divided into stations representing all the skills taught at camp. The audience is then encouraged to journey from station to station. Many parents remain with their children and watch them endlessly repeat their hard-learned skills. Then we all gather in the theater for a little Shakespeare, magic, and dance.

Our finale hasn't changed in fifteen years. Somehow everyone squeezes on stage in a pleasing arrangement and belts out our current anthems. My personal favorites are "I Am a Patriot," by Little Stephen Van Zant, "Teach Your Children," by Graham Nash, and "The World Is Coming to a Start," from

Pearlie Victorious. Not necessarily in that order. There is something that happens when that concentration of pure, unbridled energy beams out this familiar and positive message to their parents, who just bounce it back to their kids as pure and unconditional love. Then all things become possible, and there is not a dry eye on the property.

Let me close with our most recent amazement: Winnarainbow Inner Space Exploration, or WISE. WISE guys. WISE girls. WISE Gaia. It came to me up the spinal telegraph during my afternoon meditation, and I introduced it to the general population the following night after the evening program.

If any children wish to participate, they must first clear it with their counselors and then take their seats quietly on the log benches that surround the fire circle (after brushing their teeth). After about ten minutes they are led across the stream and into the eucalyptus grove, where they sit in absolute silence for a guided meditation. Any breach of that silence means instant dismissal from the circle for three nights. It was in this sweet and silent circle that I learned that kids would do almost anything to stay up later than other kids—even watch their own breath by candlelight. This was not a fad or a fluke. Some kids came every night. Most came every now and then. Repeaters were rewarded with free copies of *The Three-Minute Meditator* by David Harp. Next summer, we might levitate Laytonville. So cheer up.

Today Laytonville, tomorrow the world!

From the Ridiculous to the Sublime

Gilda Radner said it best in the guise of Emily Litella, "It's always something." You just never know what the universe is going to throw at you next. If it's not one thing, it's another.

Take December 1989. First I get this far-out invite from the Esalen Institute, home of the human potential movement, or as I call it, the encounterculture.

Esalen is located on the south coast of northern California near Big Sur. It comes complete with sea-dashed cliffs and hot smelly water. This healing spa is a sacred spot to soak away life's owies, aches, and pains. This place is so gorgeous that thousands of overqualified human beings fight to pay *beaucoup* bucks to serve as work-scholars. This enables them to bust their butts as maids or dishwashers or gardeners in exchange for a lecture, a roof, and three squares in paradise.

Then there is the staff that actually runs the joint. They get to stay for free and some of them actually receive photos of dead presidents (money) for services rendered.

My invite is for staff week, when all the paying guests and work-scholars are asked to leave, leaving only key folks alone with one another to kick back. It is a chance for them to catch a collective breath, and recharge their batteries for the coming year.

That is where I come in. I am asked to hang out, heal up, and lend some of my flavor to the Esalen soup. Well, wooga wooga—this is just de ting for this here battered old clown. So I show up and suck up the sunsets and salmon, and soak in the hot smelly water till the lumps leave the Gravy.

Now it's payback time. What can I offer this place and these people who have given me so much? The answer's as plain as the clown nose on my clown face. *Honk, honk.* A little laughter as we stagger toward the light. These caretakers of paradise get hit with a lot of psychic garbage, so I set out to hose 'em down with clown juice. An inner teaching of the First Church of Fun comes squirting to my consciousness.

If you take a paper bag that just fits over your head and do the funny mantra (which is the New Age version of the rasp-berry), it will cause the bag to vibrate and you will turn into a human kazoo. Laura Huxley said, "It works if you work." Sooo, Pphhhhhttt . . . and voila! No more bummer.

It is always very difficult for me to find the proper bag when I do this on the road. At Esalen, however, there are three perfect bags in every bathroom of every housing unit. They use them to pick up the trash. Little did they know of their sacred purpose until my Funny transmission. It was a matter of bath-room sink-ronicity.

But the true bag, the one that is perfect for your individual head, remains an individual quest. Alas, even when you find the true bag, hot air and saliva will cause it to expand with con-tinued use, so the quest for the true bag is a perpetual one. To paraphrase St. Francis of Assisi, "What is the bag but the search for the bag?"

Follow that pair o' dux as we travel down the road a piece

that passeth understanding, which next finds me riding in that highway in the sky. I'm on a flight to Mexico City to join up with my wife Jahanara, son Jordan, fellow family member Cedar, plus Sunanda and Adad from Seva Canada. All of us are in cahoots to bring a semblance of Santa Claus to the refugee camps in the Mexican state of Chiapas on the Guatemalan border.

Just flappin' your arms can be flyin' but we used Mexicana Airlines. We have seventeen bags fulla stuff, swoopin' into Tuxtela airport, where we are scooped up by Alejandra, our faithful Seva field worker from San Cristobal, which is an hour and a half uphill in our rented van.

So it's sweet dreams and blast off in the A.M. for the camps, which are down the other side of the hill another hour and a half. We left a chilly morning in the highlands to find the afternoon is an equatorial oven down below.

When we finally arrive at Camp A, I just can't believe my nose, let alone my eyes. First of all, you must understand that these refugees are Mayan Indians driven out of Guatemala by the great violence that swept through their country a few years back. The refugees are tolerated in Mexico because they provide cheap labor cutting sugar cane twelve hours a day for a handful of pesos and a flop in the mud. The shacks I visited in the other Third World countries seemed palatial compared with what these people lived in. Even their pigs looked put upon.

But the people were beautiful, with smiles like searchlights that stabbed through the squalor of every day, staying alive.

Later that day there was a meeting in Camp B, which was the most together of all the camps we visited. The meeting was held in the communal school-shed and was also attended by representatives from all the other camps that Seva was involved with.

We started out by distributing school supplies and radio

tape recorders I had panhandled from Whole Earth Access in Berkeley. These were accompanied by audio tapes of indigenous marimba music with a kicker. Then we got down to the meat of the meeting: How can we help?

All through the late afternoon, as the linear business at hand droned on and on, I was occasionally rewarded with glimpses of the huge brown eyes of the children, as they gaped in the gaps between boards. Their laughter was somehow oblivious to the hell that fate had assigned them. I think it was Kerouac or Corso who spoke of the Mexican boy "doomed" by his sombrero. Well, believe me, these kids are double doomed.

The next day was fiesta with separate celebrations scheduled for each of the camps. We started the first off with a circle, with me in my clown gear explaining the passing of a pulse. This involves a squeezing passed from hand to hand to hand around the circle—a pulse of love and hope and holy shenanigans.

Cedar and I did face-painting for the children and nary a kid did jiggle. One village did a show for us consisting of kids singing songs of sanitation. Then Adad and Jordan gave each village a performance of juggling and magic that set up the stage for the giving of gifts. Each child got one. It was categorized to their age group and was hand-wrapped by us all. It even had a tag with the child's own name on it.

The children had to be told it was okay to open their presents. This in marked contrast to the frenzy of our own kids' early unwrappings. Then, as the children and their gifts got together, we guests feasted on chicken stew (with a dash of iodine) and a flash of Fresca, while the women and elders observed our every mouthful. Then on to the next camp and the next fiesta.

At each stop, the new radios, spilled flutes, mid marimbas, and sunshine surrounded us all.

Kate Wolf's Mylar Rainbow Wig

"Wavy Gravy?" her voice gently poured out of the phone like melted chocolate. It could only be my friend Kate Wolf calling to confirm her band for my next big benefit. It was a given. Kate had furnished her own genre of homegrown northern California folk music for every Seva benefit I had ever produced (except Carnegie Hall). Seva was on a roll and so was Kate. She had a whole string of modestly successful records for the Kaleidoscope label, and had just finished taping an "Austin City Limits" television show where she received a standing ovation.

"Well, Wavy Gravy, I can't play your benefit." she whispered.

"What!" I screamed full volume, hurting my own ear.

(Pause)

"I've got leukemia," she choked.

"I don't give a @#$%&!!! I'll get you a wig."

. . . And she laughed so rich and full and loud—like a dam had burst inside her, so she couldn't hear me blubbering in the background.

It seems the cancer was spotted accidentally by her gynecologist. That explained her lack of vital energy. For the past year we had driven, once a week, the hour and a half from Berkeley to Cupertino, for chiropractic adjustments by a mutual friend. We would take turns at the wheel each way, and over the course of time Kate Wolf taught me to love a good back road.

She checked into the leukemia unit at the University of California hospital in San Francisco and started receiving massive doses of chemotherapy. On an early visit I presented her with a shiny Mylar rainbow wig and in return I was given a two-foot lock of what was once a waterfall of her beautiful brown hair. Then she asked me to ride point with her on this one, and be her hospital clown. I was ultra-honored and a little dubious. I had worked with children with leukemia for over a decade, but Kate Wolf was my first ever grown-up.

She made her hospital room into a sacred space and filled it with flowers and paintings of all outdoors. Feathers and crystals were everywhere. Things went really well in those early hospital days.

Once, though, Kate was a little bummed out, so I brought her a cuckoo clock. It's hard to maintain a bummer when a little bird jumps out of a box and hoots at you every half-hour. It worked wonders for me in my own convalescence. Whenever the cuckoo would pop out of the clock I would attempt to squirt it with my water pistol. I was so successful at this that eventually the damn thing just rusted in place.

I hung a brand new cuckoo in Kate's room with the best of intentions and returned the following day to discover she had grown these great black bags under her eyes. That damn cuckoo had kept her up all night long. Boy, was I bummed. Oh well, in the words of Werner Erhard, "You win some, you lose some."

Shortly after I removed the clock, Kate went into remission. She left the hospital and traveled to the high Sierras for some organic R&R. En route, she stopped briefly at Camp Winnarainbow with her older daughter, Hannah. Together they witnessed our winning "best in parade" at the Laytonville Old-timers Day. I still have the photos she took before returning to her beloved high country. I, in turn, boogied back to Berkeley.

Summer sizzled into autumn, which in California means Indian summer and some of the best days of the year, weather-wise. I was asked by Kate's guitarist, Nina Gerber, to come up to Nevada City and emcee a benefit that many of Kate's friends had set up to help defer her medical expenses.

The "event" was held in the great barnlike theater of the Victorian Museum. The joint was packed and overflowing with her fans. Grizzled prospectors, back-to-the-land hippies, loggers, and Earth Firsters. Kate's poems spoke to almost everyone and they all showed up for the payback. It was a pity she couldn't have been there, I thought, just to feel all the love in that hall.

The performers sure felt it, and they ladled it up in buckets, and poured it back into the house.

Before you knew it, the show was over. It was time for the finale. The words to "Give Yourself to Love" were printed on the back of the program. This was one of Kate's signature songs and all the musicians streamed on stage and joined the audience in singing along.

"Kind friends all gather round, there's something I would say . . ."

There was Nina and Ford James, The Seskins, Dakota Sid, Jonathan Richmond . . . and me plunking away on my little one-string Indian iktar.

"Give yourself to love, if love is what you're after" . . . (out of the corner of my eye I see all these other entertainers deftly slipping offstage) . . .

"Open up your heart to the tears and laughter" . . . (till there's nobody there but me).

". . . and give yourself to love" . . . (and I forgot the words to the next verse). The audience covered as I ducked behind my iktar. "Plunk, plunk, plunk!" (I was wondering what form of diabolical fiend could possibly subject me to this embarrassing situation, when out she stepped regally through the rear curtain, magnificent in her rainbow Mylar wig.)

"I just knew I'd surprise you someday, Wavy Gravy!" said Kate.

One thousand points of real light exploded from her Mylar hair.

She really got me good.

Kate Wolf died of acute leukemia in December 1986.

Good grief.

Earth People's Park

The following is a letter I dashed off in a fit of pique and sent out to my family and friends in the fall of 1990.

Dear Friends:

Around twenty years ago, the Hog Farm, in cahoots with legions of like-hearted hippies, set out to buy back the earth and give it away so it would never be for sale again. And the last places we would buy would be New York, London, Tokyo, Chicago, et cetera, to preserve as museums to show how people used to live before they knew any better.

Open meetings were held in California and New Mexico. Committees were formed to vibrate the vision, raise funds, and purchase land, land that belonged to everyone on earth. We called our vision Earth People's Park. Myself and the Hog Farm pledged to drive around America in our own caravan of buses and panhandle "spare change for the earth."

We would enter a city and advertise an

"Earth People's Party," replete with rock-and-roll and during the breaks I would get on a mike and push the park. Someone else would push a wheelbarrow with a giant plaster earth inside around the dance floor in a follow-spot, and the audience would respond by inserting cash through a slit in the North Pole. Other folks raised funds through advertising in alternative newspapers and magazines.

Back in those golden days of hippie high-jinx it seemed anything was possible. The earth was our oyster and the park was its pearl. Well, it wasn't quite that easy. Vietnam was exploding all around us and people's priorities were justly blowin' in the wind.

About thirty-five thousand had been raised for an Earth People's Park and all parties involved decided to make a purchase as soon as possible. The circumstances escape me, but it did come to pass that the money was spent to liberate 592 acres of land in the border town of Norton, Vermont. We were the last left-hand turn in America.

A board of directors was set up in California to cover external legal hassles, but it was always understood that the people living on the land at the moment would obey state laws and make up other rules as they went along. Ah, sweet Ann R. Key—long may she wobble.

Well, we are now two decades down the road and over the years countless thousands have passed through Earth People's Park. Many stayed and fashioned campsites and a few built semipermanent homes. Occasionally, in the early years, we in California would be hit on to help pay off back taxes, but less frequently as time went by.

I made several attempts to lure the Rainbow Family to Norton to build a Peace Village. The Rainbow Family is a loosely knit band of hippies who gather each year to celebrate their humanity and concern for the natural world. I felt these rainbow people would be ideal settlers if the original vision was to advance beyond a transient population.

I was getting a world-class nibble when the shit hit the fan, or in this case, the saw hit the trees. A wedge of biker-junkies moved onto the land and started to sell timber to feed their heroin habits and wallets. Anyone who objected to this turn of events was either relocated or successfully intimidated.

Tony Serra was the original Earth People's Park lawyer. He may be the most famous and flamboyant murder lawyer in the free world. (James Woods plays Tony in the film True Believer.) I told Tony what was afoot in Vermont and he freaked. Within ten minutes we had located the old EPP corporate seal (which had been missing for over a decade), and Tony dictated a heavy letter to all parties concerned with the sale of the timber in Vermont, saying in effect that this act of plunder was akin to stealing the candlesticks from the altar of a church. Copies were sent to the loggers and buyers and police and border guards and everyone else who came to mind. The logging was stopped cold and we were ecstatic. Wood that had already been cut was used to construct a much-needed bridge for the park.

While we were feeling good about ourselves, these evil assholes went about their daily business of intimidation and drug dealing. This time we're talking guns and ganja. The same dude who handled the bank account for the timber swindle was just busted selling around fifty pounds of hooch at Earth People's Park to a federal agent. The ensuing raid also uncovered a stash of firearms and over ten thousand dollars in cash. Now the feds want to seize the land.

No way. Not only are we talking natural wonder, with some of the finest swimming holes in the hemisphere, but beavers and a border. With all the heat in the Arabian desert you never know when a border will come in handy again.

Here comes the pitch. We need a pile of money to stop the seizure. We also need to transfer the board of directors to the east coast. Bring on local ex-parkers who are in touch with day-by-day park business. Rules need to be created so none of this can happen again. The park needs to be a safe haven for all life forms. No guns! No logging! No shit!

Wanna help? Make your checks payable to: Earth People's Park, c/o Richard Wilson, Trustee, 130 Bush Street, San Francisco, CA 94104.

Peace and Carrots. Dare to struggle, dare to grin.

I sent this letter to everyone on the mailing list for *Hog Callings*. That list includes family, friends, and interested parties.

Hog Callings is our expanded family's expanded newsletter. And if you would like a copy, please write to: Hog Callings, 1301 Henry Street, Berkeley, CA 94709. The first one's free.

Here's an Earth People's update: In the dead of winter we arranged for federal marshals to tag eviction notices to the shelters of the aforementioned assholes. This was absolutely necessary if we were to distance ourselves (we being the good-guy assholes) from the alleged perpetrators. If the notices were ignored we were faced with the prospect of paying the marshals to once again move into the park and forcibly remove the earth people from the park. We were spared this final indignity as they left of their own accord. Praise God! But wait: We're not out of the woods yet.

The feds requested that I fly at my own expense to the Northeast Kingdom for a federal deposition. I arrived late March in Burlington, Vermont, in a flurry of snow, rain, hail, and sleet. My old friend Roz Paine met me at the airport. I remember Roz from Woodstock and the revolution. Roz was Abbie Hoffman's tight right hand. She is now a legal investigator working for our Vermont attorney, Ms. Sandy Baird, who accompanied Roz to the runway.

At Roz's house in the stix I poured over various interrogatories and the deposition of Laura K., the ex-park resident who originally alerted us to the illicit logging. (Bless these ex-parkers who have kept it together over all these years. Without their tenacity we would have lost the place long ago.)

My own deposition took place the next day at the federal building in Burlington. The United States attorney assigned to our case behaved more like a fan than an adversary. He also sported an enormous moustache that was extremely mesmerizing, bobbing up and down as he spoke.

I drifted lazily back to that Indian summer two decades before when I first visited Earth People's Park. It was a quick

in-and-out for the summer solstice. A heavenly blur of fir trees
and running rivers. That bobbing beaver is actually the lawyer's
moustache leading me back, back . . . back to that Earth People's Party. The ticket to get in was a T-shirt designed by Robert
Crumb. It featured an extremely female yeti swinging from a
tree to the caption EARTH PEOPLE'S PARK IS READY TO BOOGIE!
The music was mostly provided by the Holy Modal Rounders
rockin' in to the darkness. I can still see the steam streaming off
their bodies in the moonlight; giving way to David Bromberg
under the stars—

"Oh, Mr. Gravy." The government guy deftly flips me
back to the present. A twenty-year time warp explodes. *Kerpow!*

My basic rap to the feds is, "I don't know nothing." Which
is basically the whole truth and nothing but it. The only time we
heard from people living at the park was early on, when they
needed our financial assistance to help pay off the taxes. In later
years the residents got it together and the park paid its own
way. I always thought Vermont was way too cold for cannabis
cultivation and was legitly shocked to find out to the contrary.

We went back and forth, this government guy and I, for
the better part of a day. I grew extremely agitated whenever I
spoke of the dudes who did in our dream for drugs and money.
I told the feds all about our collective vision of a free and open
space where new lifestyles could come into fruition. My God,
we had recycling stations in the park twenty years ago! The
trees were honored members of the community then and only
dead wood was fair game for shelters or fireplace. The minute
we heard of the clear-cutting for profit we took immediate
action and the same was true with the drug bust. The truth is
a formidable ally. So are Sandy Baird, Roz Paine, and the
ACLU.

That night we had a fundraiser at Roz's house. She

cooked up a tasty batch of spicy chicken, and I did my Earth People's pitch, which sold a pile of T-shirts for legal defense. Then we traveled down the road in a blizzard in Laura K's jeep for a four-hour haul to the Canadian border. Then I crashed for about five hours in Laura's cabin in the woods.

The next afternoon she persuaded a couple of teenagers to drive me to the park. The boy was raised on the land and his girlfriend was a cautious and competent driver. Just as well. It was slip-slidin' all the way.

Earth People's Park was a winter wonderland of newfallen snow. Whatever violation and carnage existed was buried under six inches of fluffy white stuff. The fir trees groaned with full boughs. At first it was incredibly quiet. Then, as we left the car to trudge down the unplowed road, whose pristine surface was only slightly marred by a few solitary footprints, we heard the muffled pow-pow-pow of a weapon being discharged. This put me on alert, as both Laura and I had been publicly threatened by the bad guys.

Pow-pow-pow-pow-pow-pow, as the Uzi went on automatic fire and this enormous dude stepped out of the underbrush.

"I'm the mayor," he roared.

I shit an imaginary brick as I pondered his image. It was suitably swaddled in woodsy-like gear: snowmobile boots, red-and-black-checkered hunting pants, bulky blue-hooded parka, black beard, and sunglasses on this suddenly gray afternoon.

"Don't let that shootin' spook you. That's just the farmer down the road engaging in a little target practice," reassured the mayor.

He took us to his shelter, which was recently acquired upon the eviction of the mean and nasties. This guy took pity on my wet and frozen tootsies and gave me a pair from his stash of snowmobile boots and then hit me up for assorted drugs. I said I didn't have drugs, thanked him for the boots, and beat a hasty retreat for the car. I mean, if he was the mayor I can just imagine the constituency . . .

This epic is far from over. Tony Serra has yet to be deposed. The trial, if it goes that far, will have to wait. The only bona fide seizure was the one I had when the mayor leaped out of the bushes.

It's never over till ye fat lady sings and I suspect, in this case, she ain't been born yet.

It is now the spring of '91, and the case is still in limbo. I have mellowed considerably since I composed that combination Christmas card and first angry rant for funds. In my heart of hearts I know we are all assholes and we are all Buddhas, yet even Buddha has to take a dump occasionally. So be it!

The following is the proposed text for a wooden sign to be installed at both entrances to the park:

Welcome to Earth People's Park. While you are here consider this place your home and please treat it as such. The trees are our brothers and sisters. Use only dead wood for fires and shelter. Be kind to each other and our mother the earth. Obey all state and federal laws. And show compassion for all life forms. Pack out your garbage, bury your shit. And don't forget to smile at the wonder.

Abbie Hoffman
without Tears

The Blue Plate is the unlikely name of this straight-looking, all-American tavern on the outskirts of Worchester, Massachusetts, run by a giant with the equally unlikely name of Tiny.

Tiny is also the driver and bodyguard for His Holiness the Dalai Lama. It is not unusual to find an assortment of redneck truck drivers mixed with a houseful of hippies and beatniks digging on Ginsberg or Guthrie (Arlo).

I was extremely excited about playing the Blue Plate. Tiny dutifully met my train from Manhattan at the Worchester station. We had a little time to kill, and he suggested we attend a memorial for my old friend Abbie Hoffman. Abbie had been dead for a whole year now. Time seems greased since I started sliding down the other side of fifty. It seemed like only a couple months had passed since I officiated at wakes on both coasts of America.

At the L.A. wake they used me as the hook. If folks went on too long I'd lurk in the wings in bleak and tragic clown regalia, armed with a plastic scythe and rubber sledge hammer. It seemed to do the trick. My only official hook was Paul Krassner and it was just pretend.

When the power failed during Jackson Browne, I got to

do my thing for real. Like a clown possessed I leapt into the dead air and did a gong-bong. This involved getting everyone I could con into holding hands, squatting down, hyperventilating fourteen breaths, holding the last breath, standing up and releasing it simultaneously as energy to send to Abbie on his way and to bring peace to the planet. Well, we just about took the roof off the funeral parlor.

A month later in New York City I put bags over everyone's head and read my Abbie poem, which suggests that he has gone to give Joe Hill a well-earned rest:

> *Don't mourn, organize.*
> *Go out and do something beautiful*
> *for the people or the planet*
> *and have fun doing it.*
> *Go out and win one for the Yipper!*

I concur with Jerry Rubin that Abbie would have made a great old person. And I know I'll miss him more as I enter my geezerhood.

I told Tiny to be sure to get me to the synagogue on time. I hate to be late for anything.

We sat inconspicuously in the back row. Well, inconspicuous for a rainbow-toothed clown and a giant. Unlike the Blue Plate, this was a totally straight venue. No Anita or Amerika, not even his widow Joanna, who was waked-out in the Cement Apple. I recognized his brother Jack, and his mother whom I never met.

The program began with a folk-singing rabbi, followed by an endless sermon and an equally boring and equally endless series of testimonials from the congregation. The entire proceeding was extremely formal and extremely serious. I began to wonder just who they were talking about. It was giving me major chest pains. The Abbie they evoked bore no resemblance to anyone I ever knew.

The pain in my chest grew stronger and stronger. It was as if a giant bird had clawed its way through my chest and was squeezing my heart with its talons. When I could bear it no longer I leaped up and started spewing out my own Abbie stories. Stories about how he ignited a generation with his antics. About how he used humor as a weapon against the war in Vietnam. I told them about the time we spent together backstage at the moratorium in Washington, D.C.

Nearly a million people had gathered to say no to our military involvement in Southeast Asia. We had this giant plat-form stage set up and the P.A. was supplied by Bill Hanley, the guy who did the sound for the Woodstock music festival. On stage was Pete Seeger, who was doing a successful singalong with this enormous audience.

"All we are saying is give peace a chance. All we are saying" . . . when from out of nowhere stepped Mitch Miller of "Sing Along With Mitch," a mainstream pop television show, who exhorted the audience to "Give me a sea of V's."

"All we are saying is give peace a chance," sang the crowd as they swayed back and forth, flashing their V's.

"All we are saying . . ."

And Abbie Hoffman leaned over and whispered in my already incredulous ear, "They got Norman Luboff in the wings . . ."

". . . is give peace a chance."

I knew he was putting me on. Norman Luboff was the conductor of a violin orchestra á la Montovani and wouldn't deign to appear within a hundred miles of this event, but I went for it anyway.

"All right!" I exclaimed. "Middle America has taken over

the peace movement. We can retire. We don't have to do this stuff anymore."

At that moment, a hundred doves were released to fly heavenward with prayers for peace. In route, one of them shit on my third eye.

"There's your answer," Abbie hooted. "We can never stop doing it."

How I wished he had taken his own good advice as I continued my testimony to the Abbie I knew. I only had brief glimpses into the darkness of his demise. His sunny side, however, seemed always up and busy. From floating money over the balcony at the New York Stock Exchange in the sixties or extolling us in the eighties to mail our urine samples to the White House, he was the clown prince of the counterculture and the inspiration for my invective, "Dare to struggle . . . dare to grin!"

No sooner had I finished speaking than the talons were withdrawn from my heart and I could breathe again. After a moment of silence came the laughter and applause. His mom even walked me out to the foyer for coffee and cake. Brother Jack said he'd phone me up for an interview for this book he was working on.

Then Tiny expertly steered me out the door and into the smooth leather embrace of his limo, which sped us silently through the snow.

That's the Bag I'm In

It is indeed a wonder that a simple slab of tree flesh can deliver such dramatic results. Once I did a workshop on humor and disability by the bay. My first task was to get those wheelchairs in a circle and sing a couple choruses of "Harpo's Ladder" (sung to the tune of "Jacob's Ladder"). This is a song I wrote and dedicated to my guru Harpo Marx and my friend John Brent. I accompany myself on a one-string instrument called the iktar.

It's a singalong, so as you read it, sing it in your head starting with the chorus.

> *We are climbing Harpo's Ladder*
> *We are climbing Harpo's Ladder*
> *Just an opera hat full of yellow chickens*
> *He was a soldier of the clowns*
> *Soldier, do you love my cream pies?*

At this point I get people to pick up an imaginary three-pound pie, decide if it is coconut, strawberry, chocolate, key lime, et cetera, and commit pie-a-cide or smush said pie in their neighbor's face, and lick each other off. In the case of the workshop, a lot of the tossing and licking was done by attendants.

And sing with me:

Soldier, do you love my cream pies
Sacred implements of the clowns

(Chorus)

Soldier do you love my whoopie

Here I do the funny mantra (Pppphhhhhttttttt!) and encourage the audience to follow suit, explaining how my guru Harpo Marx suggests that if you are on a bummer and all else fails, stand on your head. Well, this was out of the question for the folks in the wheelchairs so we whipped out the paper bags, slipped them over our heads, did the Funny Mantra, and turned ourselves into human kazoos, and with a great blast of oral flatulence dissolved into light and laughter. Then we finished the song:

Soldier, do you love my whoopie

(Pphhhh! and rise up in your chair when you make that noise.)

Soldier, do you love my whoopie
Sacred cushion of the clowns!

(Chorus)
Last time, with gusto . . .

And look around the room. Disabled brothers and sisters are sprawled everywhere, howling with the healing laughter of life.

Some patients refused to remove their bags at bedtime. The doctors in attendance collected a whole stash of bags to use at their board meeting later that evening.

I began to integrate my gospel of the bag into my rounds at the children's hospitals—working one on one with the kids, slipping a bag under every pillow. The next day the nurses told me that most kids truly waited till the apex of their depression, then out came the bag and almost always a chuckle.

We printed the programs to my fiftieth birthday benefit at the Berkeley Community Theater on white paper bags that just slipped over your head, and I got to sing "Harpo's Ladder" with the Wavettes.

The *Pphhhtt* was resounding, but the engineers forgot to mike the audience so on the album the farts were added electronically in Baltimore.

Someday, I'll re-record it using live *Pphhhtt's*. Meanwhile, move over Milli Vanilli.

The Garden Club

Proposed text for a lecture to be delivered to the ladies' horticultural society:

Good afternoon, ladies and gentlemen:

The Eskimos of Canada and Alaska have fifty words for snow. The hippies and potheads of North America have at least as many for hemp. I compiled this particular list while emceeing the afternoon's entertainment at the First International Exposition of Hemp held at the prodigious Hall of Flowers in San Francisco's Golden Gate Park in the spring of 1991.

Creating this list seemed a pleasant way to interact with the audience in between stories, songs, and speeches. During the breaks, folks would call out their choices for the hemp hall of fame and I would add them to the list. Where that list is today is anybody's guess. Herein lies my own modest recollection.

Acapulco gold	bhang
Amuska Valley	bong

boo	marijuana
bowl	marrahoochie
bread	Mary Jane
bricks	Maui wowie
bud	Missouri mud
bush	Mr. Green
dagga	muggles
doobie	Panama red
dope	pot
gage	reefer
ganja	sensemilla
grass	shit
hash	smoke
hemp	spliff
herb	stuff
joint	tama
kif	tea
kind	THC
lambs	the green
leaf	thunderfuck
ma	weed

I had a high old time at the Hall of Flowers, networking with my fellow hempsters, attending conferences on horticulture and legalization, and visiting the many booths. There were vendors of hemp fashion and dispensers of hemp information. Organizations like NORML (the National Organization for the Reform of Marijuana Laws) and HEMP (Help Eliminate Marijuana Prohibition) were very much present.

The surprise of the morning was the serving of hemp pancakes.

A banquet held that evening featured a cavalcade of tasty treats. I particularly enjoyed the hemp mayonnaise for the artichokes, and the chocolate almond hemp torte; the hemp loaf I found rather bland and tasteless.

The pièce de résistance were keynote speeches by a San Francisco city supervisor and a candidate for the governorship of Kentucky. This was a far cry from my early encounters with the "deadly herb" in the somnambulant late fifties.

As a young poet I helped initiate jazz and poetry to the east coast. Imagine my horror when I discovered that members of my band were "using" marijuana. I remember both my horror and their amusement as I tried to dissuade these musicians from destroying their lives. My points of reference at the time were limited to yellowed *Life* magazine photos of a furtive and sleepy-eyed Robert Mitchum, freshly flushed from a motel room by police in the forties and what I had heard throughout my middle-class childhood, which was next to nothing at all.

My personal initiation to pot came that summer in Kennebunkport, Maine, where, after smoking, I covered an entire automobile with shaving cream and laughed for almost a week. When I finally calmed down, my anonymous drummer took me aside and explained the intricacies of the marijuana subculture—i.e., how to be "cool."

I learned that if I got caught "holding" or smoking marijuana I could get in big trouble. He showed me how to "stash," or hide my stuff, and to always lock the door, and place a bath towel on the floor between the door and the floor before I smoked.

He also recommended incense or room freshener to take away the incriminating odor. In those days you could do big time for a little grass. Five years for a single stick of "boo" was not uncommon. During the early sixties it was not considered paranoid to keep a bucket of water by the toilet bowl and have the tap water running slightly all night long. Just before a dawn raid the police would cut off your water supply, which would allow you only one flush for destruction of evidence. Then they would burst through the door and go for your throat. This, to prevent you from swallowing what you were unable to flush.

Sound farfetched? Not really. It's all a question of geography. Where I live, in Berkeley, being caught in possession of under an ounce of pot is something like a parking ticket. In fact, twenty-seven states, containing roughly three-quarters of the United States population, have voted to decriminalize. But if you are in Arizona, New Mexico, or Nevada, you could do three years for simple possession. Growers in some states face more time than convicted murderers.

As part of the war on drugs, an entire northern California town was held hostage by members of C.A.M.P. in a joint operation (no pun intended) with U.S. troops and members of the Colombian army, while they looked for fields of pot plants.

It kind of makes you wonder what the fuss is all about. We are discussing a comparatively innocent herb whose recreational smoking can cause some bronchitis and the munchies. Alcohol- and tobacco-related deaths number nearly half a million. Stoned motorists tend to be over-careful and drive too slow. Some people smoke way too much. In moderation, however, marijuana can be both expanding to the senses and refreshing to the soul. I find a small amount of marijuana before yoga and meditation adds impetus to my spiritual attainment. It has been labeled by its detractors as a gateway drug. In my own case it is a gateway to God.

Now, wait just a minute, Gravy. Enough with the God stuff. Forget the pleasure of recreational marijuana use for a minute. Don't even mention the enormous revenue that could be generated by legalization and taxation of one of the largest cash crops on the planet today. Never mind about saving our schools, bailing out the S&Ls, or helping the homeless recover from the HUD scandal. Let's have none of that shit. (Sirs, Ladies, please excuse my French, but I get so passionate.)

Let us consider instead that hemp has served for centuries as a purveyor of fine paper products. Some strains reach a height of twenty feet in a year and don't even get you high. Why not grow and harvest this harmless product in lieu of the destruction of our remaining old-growth forests? Our founding fathers grew hemp for rope, canvas, and paper. There were sixty tons of hemp used on the U.S. Constitution alone. Old Ironsides and Old Glory proved hemp a worthy fabric. In fact, hemp is softer, stronger, warmer, and more water absorbent than cotton, and, unlike cotton, does not depend on toxic pesticides to grow. I am wearing my 50 percent stoned-ground blue hemp sport shirt as I speak. It is approximately two years old and has experienced repeated washing. I just love it.

Okay, let's skip this stuff about Old Glory, God, and my blue shirt. Let's talk biomass. As opposed to fossil fuels, which are nonrenewable resources, biomass is a renewable living vegetation that, in this case, readily converts to methanol, which is the fuel of choice of the Indianapolis 500.

Okay, now park that car, and keep your shirt off. Even ignore global warming, which could be averted by the saving of the rainforests and the generous infusion of the hemp plant on a planetary basis.

If that is not enough inducement for a renaissance of reefer, let us at least take mercy on the victims of glaucoma. *Cannabis sativa* is effective in lowering ocular pressure, yet it must now be obtained by illegal means. Hey, the American Medical Association has just stated that marijuana is the best agent for the control of nausea in cancer chemotherapy. Even so, the cries of the terminally ill and their advocates still fall on seeming deaf ears for a lessening of the strict federal and state controls on the medical uses of marijuana.

What the hell is going on here, anyway? I don't believe the United States is all that worried about my health and welfare as a result of cannabis consumption. In fact I'll stake my stash and paraphernalia it has something to do with money and control— or in a word, *capitalism,* and our old friend the military-industrial complex.

It really blows my mind that my allies on this issue are the likes of William F. Buckley, Jr., who wants to legalize *all* drugs just to take away the profit motive. No profit, no crime. No crime, no criminals.

However, I believe there is a big difference between crack, smack, and smoking flowers. Not until we define our drugs instead of lumping them all together, and not until young people are told the truth about each specific substance, will we see less drug-related teenage death.

So I'm begging you, ladies and gentlemen, here and now, on behalf of your children and their schools and the trees and the sick, the infirm and the homeless, and the cold and huddling masses yearning to be stoned.

For the sake of our planet, our cars, and our quest for communion with our creator, let us all pledge to work for the legalization of marijuana, cannabis, hemp, pot, reefer, leaf, Mary Jane, boo, muggles, et cetera.

I would like to see it sold in our stores as an alternative to alcohol, and taxed accordingly, and restricted to consumers at least eighteen years old. These revenues should be distributed in every state and spent on education, health care, and housing. Lest the government hold that bake sale to pay for their B-1 bombers, I also believe that each citizen should be permitted to grow, tax free, one yard in their yard.

Does all this resemble science fiction? Well, it wasn't all that long ago we were machine-gunning each other in the streets over alcohol. When Prohibition was finally lifted, the money went from the gangsters to the government, and the gin moved out of the bathtubs and into the liquor stores.

Why? Because registered voters demanded it. Alcohol is much more dangerous than hemp. I don't think you can find a medical doctor on the planet who will disagree with me on that point. Nicotine is far more toxic and deadly. What a blessing it would be if this nation's tobacco fields could re-tool for reefer. And what a boon to those financially depressed Southern states.

Each day we move a little closer to legalization. I can just feel it in my bones. Cannabis, incidentally, is a proven remedy for arthritis and rheumatism when used as a poultice. I appeal to you to clear the way for your horticultural skills to move beyond the beauty of the rose, and to embrace new horizons in hemp.

Its buds are not without their beauty, as I discovered this past winter when I spoke at a convention in Indianapolis entitled "Hemp at the Hilton." My opening speech was followed by an illuminating slide presentation by acclaimed author and botanist Ed Rosenthal. His syndicated column of gardening tips, "Just Ask Ed," is read by hundreds of thousands of Americans each month. Honestly, you just had to be there. The sight of those beautiful buds under extreme magnification with their many shades of green and gold (to accentuate the wonder of those delightful purple hairs) caused me to join with the audience in an eruption of appreciative applause. In between images Mr. Rosenthal would field pertinent questions from the farmers on the floor concerning irrigation, fertilizer, and the like.

The event was partially sponsored by HEAD—Hoosiers Embarrassed About Dan—and HEMP. Hemp needs your help. Write your elected representatives and demand the deregulation of all non-smoking commercial use of hemp. Insist on its

prescribed medical usage, ask for re-legalization of private personal consumption and minimal cultivation, and for state regu-
lation of the marijuana industry as in alcohol and tobacco.

Talk to friends, family, and co-workers about the non-
narcotic properties of hemp. Donate your time and money to
organizations working for its legalization. The time is now!

Let my people grow!

Thank you for your time and your attention. Now, let us
adjourn to the patio for tea and cucumber sandwiches.

You too, sir.

The Sacred Shit List

There is a piece of paper floating around out there in the world with a life of its own, changing and reproducing itself at the whims of creation. This contemporary phenomenon lies somewhere between *Everything I Need to Know I Learned in Kindergarten* and *The Rocky Horror Picture Show*. The former for its reproductive prowess between the pulpit and the page, and the latter for its ever-changing litany between its audiences across America and the actors on the screen.

This toothy slab of tree flesh keeps popping up everywhere I go these days. In various incarnations, I have found it stuck under my windshield wiper in New England, shoved under the door in Indiana, and stuck in my hand last week at the Whole Earth Festival in Davis, California. In my other hand was a working microphone so, naturally, I read it aloud. The audience loved it. Several people asked me for copies. So many, in fact, that I have decided to include it here. This piece is, like ourselves, a real work in progress, so feel free to both circulate and amend as I have done by changing the title from "A Short Guide to Comparative Religions" to "The Sacred Shit List."

Taoism	Shit happens.
Confucianism	Confucius say, "Shit happens."
Calvinism	Shit happens because you don't work hard enough.
Buddhism	If shit happens, it really isn't shit.
Seventh Day Adventist	No shit on Saturdays.
Zen	What is the sound of shit happening?
Hedonism	There's nothing like a good shit happening.
Hinduism	This shit happened before.
Mormon	This shit is going to happen again.
Islam	If shit happens, it is the will of Allah.
Moonies	Only happy shit really happens.
Stoicism	This shit is good for me.
Protestantism	Let the shit happen to someone else.
Catholicism	Shit happens because you are bad.
Hare Krishna	Shit happens, rama rama.
Judaism	Why does this shit always happen to *us?*
Zoroastrianism	Shit happens half the time.

Christian Science	Shit is in your mind.
Atheism	Sheeit.
Existentialism	What is shit, anyway?
Rastafarianism	Let's smoke this shit.

On my most current shit list, the Taoist line has been changed to "Shit flows." In that case I am sure Confucius say "Shit Flows." In a still earlier edition the Mormon "This shit is going to happen again" was replaced by "If shit happens, you got a lotta wives to blame it on," or, my own "Sheep happens." Paul Krassner says in Iran, "Shiite Happened." I would also like to add my two-word definition of history: "Shit Happened." Deep shit, no doubt about it.

It is the sacred task of the intuitive clown to turn shit into fun. This is the ultimate alchemy to which I am called. It is my chosen task to toss the tender turds of time into the dancing fan of our existence.

But not without your help, so please give a shit . . . take a shit . . . give a shit . . . give two shits . . . give shit a chance . . . is there no end to this shit? . . . this shit is bound for glory, this shit . . .

This shit has gone far enough . . . shit for brains . . . you can't tell shit from shinola . . . don't try and shit me . . . the eagle shit on Friday. . . . I'm talking some real shit.

Good shit . . . bad shit . . . stupid shit . . . just who do you think you're shittin' . . . shit or git off the pot . . . cheap shit . . . expensive shit . . . shit out of luck . . . lucky shit . . . dipped in shit . . . shit or go blind . . . eat shit . . . shoot the shit . . . straight shit . . . shit-faced . . . shit canned . . . shit on a stick . . . shit-eating grin . . . horse shit . . . bullshit . . . built like a brick shithouse.

*   *   *

Hot shit . . . and holy shit.

To be continued . . .

Am I Experienced?

I was innocently ambling down West 8th Street in the Village one evening in the early sixties when I found myself sandwiched between David Crosby and Al Kooper. As we walked they slipped a pair of headphones over my ears and stood back to enjoy my reaction.

"Well, what do you think?" asked the Cos.

"It sounds like World War Five," was the best reply I could muster at that moment. My mind was on fire and smoke was pouring out of my ears. I had just experienced Jimi Hendrix for the first time.

Nietzsche once said, "You must have chaos in your heart to give birth to a dancing star." Well, change the heart to the head and the stars will come out shooting.

Jimi Hendrix was jamming at the Gaslight with John Hammond, Jr., and one time I got to hang out after the gig.

We moved the late-night scene to this warehouse on the Hudson River where I witnessed Hendrix and Eric Clapton swapping electric licks into the dawn.

Almost thirty years later I have attempted to impart some of those sacred audio transmissions to the kids at Camp Winnarainbow. We have a ten-year tradition going that on the last morning of each camp session we slap Jimi's version of "The Star-Spangled Banner" on the huge P.A.

One moment they are sweetly sleeping in their teepees and the next they are levitated at least six inches in their sleeping bags. At the rocket's red glare, their little ears begin to smoke, and as bombs burst in the air they gather wide-eyed on the grass.

"What was that, Wavy Gravy, *World War Five?*"

It was eventually a whole lot of children who put my transcendental encounters with the power of live music in a more pastoral perspective. Peace Sunday was the single most star-studded event I ever attended in my fifty-odd years on the planet, and it also provided my main musical fix of the eighties. The event was organized by Graham Nash with a lot of help from his friends, like Stevie Wonder, Bob Dylan, John Baez, Crosby, Stills, and (naturally) Nash, Stevie Nicks . . . the list was endless. Interspersed between the bands was a potpourri of celebrities like Harrison Ford and Muhammed Ali.

Peace Sunday was held in the Rose Bowl and somehow I was chosen to lead a parade of about two thousand kids to kick off the afternoon's festivities. With this task in mind, my marching orders snapped into focus like lemon juice on a hot radiator. The infusion of dead presidents (money) by a patron of my instincts made my purchase of two thousand kazoos a reality.

We gathered with the children shortly after sunrise in peaceful Pasadena. With the able assistance of a handful of Los Angeles Hog Farmers, I began to paint posters and faces as fast as they arrived. It was an incredible ordeal. Two thousand children do tend to be a handful and I was really relieved when Tom Campbell motioned us to assume parade formation in the tunnel leading into the Rose Bowl proper.

It was then that I handed out the kazoos. The din that transpired easily eclipsed Jimi Hendrix's World War Five and

"The Star-Spangled Banner" put together. Yet out of that collective chaos, not Nietzsce but Lennon emerged to take over the tune.

We all felt him together and two thousand kazoos became one giant plea to "Give Peace a Chance."

We played it again and again in that tunnel and the sound of our prayer traveled out to the four directions imploring our ancestors to attend and to witness.

"All We Are Saying . . ."

By the time we were actually given our cue to enter the stadium we had achieved critical goosebumps and every hair on our bodies stood out in rigid attention. As we spilled out onto the playing field the familiar melody merged with the sunshine and the cheers. Then the great crowd lifted its collective larynx and joined us in that simple invocation:

> *All We Are Saying*
> *Is Give Peace a Chance.*
> *All We Are Saying . . .*

That afternoon's affair was a major Who's Who in the annals of rock-and-roll and some incredible music was shared. More star-studded than Woodstock, Peace Sunday was there just for the moment. There was no major motion picture or world satellite television spectacular. Agents and contracts forbade all such filming and tapes.

But all the stars in the firmament of rock-and-roll couldn't eclipse that time in the tunnel when John Lennon's ghost came down and took over our hearts, our minds, and our kazoos.

Imagine.

The First Church of Fun

Long ago and not so far away, in those awesome ancient times of yesteryear I helped to form a new world religion called the First Church of Fun. It was created as a reprieve from the war in Vietnam, and a bizarre concept I had of creating a clown underground to work toward the closure of same. A flyer was drawn by cartoonist Dan O'Neill of Odd's Bodkins fame, announcing our first event.

Our church was held within the respectable and imposing edifice of the First Unitarian Church, which we wheedled with the help of Paul Sawyer, the former Prankster preacher.

Our flyer promised several swell Bay Area bands, and a pair of tap-dancing penguins. I don't know what made me come up with penguins on the program. They just sort of stumbled off the extreme edge of my frontal lobe, and O'Neill popped 'em on the poster. They were already out there, so I felt compelled to deliver. Much to my chagrin, I discovered that tap-dancing penguins were a thing of the past. I learned this from the director of Sea World, no less. It seems penguins learned to tap dance when they heated up the special metal floor. Obviously, live penguins these days were out of the question. The day was saved by a couple of great gay tap dancers slipping on their penguin suits and getting down.

Karl Kohen, who teaches film at San Francisco State, brought reels of funny films like Abbott and Costello's sacred litany *Who's On First?* and *The Laughing Gas Trilogy* with Betty Boop. The all-time far-out funny flick was brought by the great cartoonist, Gilbert Shelton (Wonder Warthog and The Fabulous Furry Freak Brothers). It showed how he put on a chicken suit and drove to Washington, D.C., and as the title suggests, *Set My Chickens Free,* which was also set to music and released as a single.

Now, while everybody is grooving on these movies or just enjoying the rock-and-roll, the Altered Boy begins to tie a small string around the right big toe of all those who wished to be initiated into the church and take refuge in the dodo.

That's me. I am the Divine Dodo of the First Church of Fun. My main function is to wander through the crowd with my dodo head firmly in place and wield a giant net, which I would wiggle at the wallets of the faithful, while going, *"Dough, dough, dough"* and people would toss in assorted photos of dead presidents and help us pay our expenses. Our balloon bill alone was astronomical.

By now a fair number of toes have been tied, causing their proud owners to line up on the far left side of the cathedral and await the inner teaching. One by one, each initiate was allowed to enter the back room; and as it suggested in the flyer, ''Kneel and suck the light.''

While you were sucking this giant plastic lightbulb full of sacrament, Dope Peter the six and seven eighths (that's his hat size), who was wearing an electric suit that was flashing on and off and a pair of shades with windshield wipers flapping over his eyes, would whisper the first half of The Joke.

Then the aforementioned initiate would be deftly guided to the Fallen Archbishop, Green Goddess, or Altered Girl, who would teach them the funny handshake and deliver the second half of The Joke. At that sublime moment they became "Funnies" for one year.

Every year we hold these Funny rites on the first of April. Our venues are a tad more modest but the ritual remains the same, with the sole exception of The Joke, which changes year to year. I am tempted to reveal a few old Jokes but fear excommunication. But after all, I am the dodo and where's the harm?

QUESTION: *What's old and yellow and smells like Ginger?*
ANSWER: *Fred Astaire.*

QUESTION: *What's gray and yellow and is very very dangerous?*
ANSWER: *Shark-infested custard.*

QUESTION: *What's the difference between shit and broccoli?*
ANSWER: *George Bush won't eat broccoli. (This was revised from the original, "What's the difference between buggers and broccoli?" "Kids won't eat broccoli.")*

During the early seventies we also requested our initiates to employ a sense of humor in their opposition to the war.

I trust this is also true today. War is no fun . . . ever.

It is our sacred duty to always pie for peace!

So far the inner teaching of the Funnies has been limited to cuckoo clocks and paper bags occasionally slipped over the head to beat away the bummers and the blues.

It has come to pass, however, that I have lately experienced the cosmic tickle of fresh revelation in the sacred name of Fun. Verily, it came unto me as I performed my daily bends and stretches. It came to me as I was kneeling with my head upon the ground in sweet surrender to the silly sunshine on my butt. It came to me, and then I simply mooned the sun. As sweet golden rays beamed down on my holy hole (where the sun has never shined before), I said the holy Haaaaa Haaaaa Ha Ha Ha Haaaaa! and disappeared.

It was extremely clear that all sacred mooning of the sun should be done in private, with only the faintest possibility of being busted. *(Can you get busted for buns?)* This, to enter the element of surprise into the practice. What if an entire roomful of Funnies were mooning the sun and the cops came crashing in?

Our eyes are closed. (It is extremely important to close your eyes at the mooning of the sun or the sunlamp, if the ceremony is held indoors.) Spiritual clowns could prowl the congregation and pie the peekers. The mooning should last no longer than three minutes. An egg timer would provide a perfect reminder to put away your buns and get on with the rest of the funny business, while our lawyers dealt with the police.

A funny thing came into my head the other day as I was illuminating my asshole. Nothing is not sacred. On my way to worship *Nothing* I wrote this little prayer. I call it the "Ode to the Intuitive Clown":

> *O God,*
> *please*
> *have fun*
> *with me*
> *today.*
> *Hey, man,*
> *hey pat my ham*

I give franks
I give pranks
I give up.

Lettuce all have fun together on the full moon nights that lie before us in the nineties. See you in the funnies.

By the light of the silvery moon.

Bubbles
Are Forever

I'm forever blowing bubbles. Small wonder, bubbles are the right-hand appendage of the practicing intuitive clown. Karl Malden has his American Express card, and me? I've got bubbles—and I don't leave home without 'em. Bubbles, kazoo, and red rubber clown nose. Just tuck 'em somewhere in your stuff and occasions will present themselves for their deployment. Especially bubbles. Pretty bubbles in the air.

Great big bubbles are produced with the aid of a kiddie pool full of Joy, Dawn, or similar liquid soap. Add a stiff jigger of glycerine for longer-lasting bubbles. Then simply dip a hula hoop with handles into the mixture and slip over a friend's head. It is big fun to stand inside a giant partial bubble. Upon immersion, if you would jump gently into the air, the bubble might complete itself. I myself have been unsuccessful at achieving bubblehood. Nor do I understand the mathematics that explain Tom Noddy's bubble cube, or the many other amazing configurations I have witnessed with my own eyes. It is enough to know that scientists have studied bubbles up the yin-yang. So, like the other children of the world, I'm strictly in it for the wonder.

Often in my role as children's hospital clown I use a blast

of bubbles like a surgeon would a scalpel to cut through a child's tears. This works even when children have been crying so long they have completely forgotten their initial provocation and find themselves lost on a loop of sorrow.

Suddenly the air is raining bubbles. Little bubbles. Big bubbles. Pop! Pop! Pop! Poppoppoppoppop!

"Where did those bubbles go to, Wavy Gravy?"

"Chasing children's tears. Wanna help me blow some more?"

It is a near impossibility to simultaneously blubber and blow bubbles. After much public success at distracting children while the nurses gave a shot, the doctors began to seek me out for tear control, and it soon got out of hand. I had to draw the line somewhere. The thought of a generation of kids grabbing their arms and screaming at the sight of some clown's bubbles was more than I could bear. So I had to draw the line beyond which my bubbles would not bend. No shots, no IVs, no needles in general.

Don't blow too many bubbles. Try to avoid overexposure. In time you will begin to develop a sense of when to blow or not to blow. Also, in time you will learn that each bubble is sacred, and a manifestation of the divine. One should never, never take one's bubbles for granted.

This I learned in great detail on the other side of the world. I may have been the first clown to take his bubbles trekking in Nepal. A single waft would summon up a hundred cheering children. They would chase these soapy orbs for hours—indeed, until the setting sun came burning down the snow-white Himalayas, turning ice to gold.

I was blowing bubbles in the sunset one golden afternoon at a tiny Tibetan lamasery somewhere on the side of Annapurna. The lamas were inside industriously praying for the salvation of all sentient beings. I was outside in the courtyard mesmerized by the chanting and blowing bubbles for my new friend, Lop Sang. Lop Sang was an apprentice monk who had shaved his head and donned the saffron robes of piety. He must have been all of eleven years old. Tiny glaciers twinkled in his eyes. We were both admiring the sunset reflected in this one particular bubble when the head lama stepped into the courtyard, gazed at the bubble in question, and fell to his knees.

In an instant he was upright and escorting me into the temple. Once inside, I was seated on a comfortable cushion and fed a bowl of Tibetan oatmeal, *tsampa,* swimming in water buffalo milk with just a dab of yak butter. *Yum.*

When I finished yumming they started humming and I sort of hummed along. This went on for hours and when we finally stopped the hum went on without us. I rose up in a state of utter bliss and floated towards the door, stopping only to hand the bubbles off to Lop Sang. The head lama snatched the bubbles away from the kid and placed them on the altar.

It was translated to me that on high holy days, they would blow *one* bubble for Buddha.

My Seamy Underbelly

All right! Enough already! Let's take a break from this laughter and light. Who was it who said if you want to give light you have to be willing to burn a little? That's a heavy light, Jim. Shine it over this way. Let's light up the seamy underbelly of the clown.

I think I can safely say I was stark nuts from around 1972 to 1977. Those five years following my final spinal fusion are a blur of opiates, barbituates, steroids, and you name it. It used to take me two Percodans just to get out of bed and I only slept once every three days 'cuz it hurt so much to wake up. Needless to say, I got a hell of a lot done.

Sometimes I was even incandescent. Especially in New York City. In California, people used to worry about me and how I never slept. In New York it went completely unnoticed.

I was occupying the Yippie headquarters at Bleecker Street and Bowery. The place was a total mess, with a major infestation of giant roaches when I first moved in. Instead of calling an exterminator I built the roaches an excellent amusement park, complete with see-saws, Ferris wheels, and a river of honey. The roaches were having a great time and relinquished the rest of the apartment.

I was in town warming up for the Richard Nixon Impeachment Rally to be held in Washington, D.C., the following month. I had been asked to emcee the rally and whenever I left Yippie headquarters, these two FBI guys would follow me around New York. I really enjoyed the attention and eventually I got into this ritual of hitting the Bowery disguised as a hunchback with assorted costumes in my hunch. I got so I could change identities as I walked, and learned to lose them at will.

I was also extremely occupied with raising money for RAINS—Relief for Africans in Need in the Sahel. Odetta turned me on to this loose-knit affiliation of black church groups attempting to stem the tide of famine. I called my friend Stewart Brand of *The Whole Earth Catalogue* to get some perspective.

Stuart had organized Life Raft Earth to bring attention to the possibility of world famine back in 1968. He called my attention to the then-current issue of *Fortune* magazine. Sure enough, there was a piece on the desertification of the Sahel and its impact on the global economy. The next comprehensive piece on the famine appeared in the *Wall Street Journal.* The flow of information in America—or for that matter the planet Earth—is intertwined with who's got the money.

I don't know why this came as such a shock, but when it wore off I made my move: An end run to the New York *Daily News.* I got word of this impending famine from *Fortune* and the *Journal* and circumnavigated *The New York Times,* the New York *Post,* and the *Christian Science Monitor* to place it in the entertainment section of the *News.*

This was an amazing achievement, when you consider my appearance and psychic state. I walked into Ernie LeGrande's office at the *News* wearing a rainbow-patched jumpsuit, jester's cap, a bell, the iktar at the ready, and a tiny suitcase full of weirdness. I had arranged for RAINS to reap the proceeds of the east coast premiere of the Rolling Stone's new film, *Ladies and Gentlemen . . . The Rolling Stones.*

That's how I got into Ernie's office. He took one look at my cuckoo visage and locked the door. I opened up my suitcase and started to crank up the four elements, earth, air, fire, and water, which were a rock, a canteen, a candle. Mr. LeGrande insisted on taking the stick of smoking incense I used to honor the air and hold it up to the air vent in the ceiling. He said he was doing this to keep his editor from thinking he was doing something strange. In my own crazed state this explanation made a kind of sense (although his editor might question why he was standing on his desk during our interview).

Meanwhile, all I did was pass on the famine data, which I laid at his feet along with a couple choruses of "Basic Human Needs." My mission accomplished, I started packing up to leave when Ernie climbed down from his desk and shook my hand. He said he'd worked at the *Daily News* for more than twenty years and thought he had seen everything. He wished to amend that statement. He said, "You're the strangest thing I've ever seen—and that's a compliment."

I took it as such, along with my leave. I had miles to go, promises to keep. At the rate I was going I thought I might never sleep again.

That night would kick off the weekend Anarchist Convention at Hunter College and I wanted to use the event to tighten my chops for the upcoming impeachment rally in D.C. They showed Fritz Lang's *Metropolis,* after which I politely declined an invitation from the Yippies to help them trash McDonald's.

Instead, I stayed behind and somehow convinced the janitor to let me arrange the garbage in the main hall. I explained how I was to deliver the keynote lecture on the following morning on the impact of garbage on the culture.

It was just before dawn when I finished arranging all the chairs into a giant helix, butting against a wall that contained both a water fountain and an electrical outlet. From the janitor

I got a drum on wheels to fill with imaginary trash. It had a big number 8 on its side, which for me contained overtones of infinity. The janitor said it came from the eighth floor. I turned it wheels up and wrote this note: "Please don't touch the garbage, love Nobody."

Then I staggered off to cop some z's and gather my props. When I returned it was nearly noon. I got about three hours' sleep and two hundred pounds of props.

When I arrived, the place was totally surrounded by fire engines and police who informed me there was a possible bomb in the basement. Just as I received this information I caught the eye of my old friend the janitor, who was both winking wildly and holding open a side door through which I slipped in unnoticed.

It is a hop, skip, and a jump from there to the scene of my evening's earlier handiwork. I quickly set up my base of operations at the water fountain and electrical outlet. My props included a tent and sleeping bag, flashlight, a small public address system, and a change of clothes. I shed my worksuit and began to adjust the electrodes on my dorsal column stimulator. This is a bizarre electrical device, about the size of an electric razor but covered with brown leather and studded with two metal knobs, which are used to regulate the pulse and strength of the electrical signal it delivers to my lower back through a network of wires.

I am standing there adjusting the energy, which confused the pain signals to my brain. I am naked except for the wires running into my spine, when in walks the bomb squad, who took one look at me and froze in their tracks.

The terror in their eyes said it all. I had merely to place my fingers on the metal knob of my stimulator to take total charge of the situation. "Gentlemen. That's quite close enough," I muttered menacingly.

They became statues, barely breathing.

"Back out slowly and leave me alone!"

They needed no second invitation. Upon their hasty retreat I continued dressing and arranging my stuff. In about fifteen minutes a diminutive figure appeared at the door to the auditorium.

"Hugh, are you all right?" It was Judith Malina of the Living Theater.

"We're all naked upstairs," she continued. It was clear she was sent as a representative of the powers that be and it was also clear that she suspected I was insane. Perhaps she thought I could go off at any minute. I was tempted to play this one all the way out for Judith.

"I remember when I first came to New York City and how I went to see this play called *The Connection*. I remember during the intermission the actors panhandled the audience for spare cash, which they spent on the heroin they shot up on stage during the second act."

"You mean, all this time you are doing *theater?*" she gasped. I flashed my best conspiratorial smile and then she got it. Crazy, yes . . . but not insane.

I really like it that I was the bomb scare at the Anarchist Convention.

Health Angels

The quivering wisp of a middle-aged clown sat shuddering in his seat while he absorbed the good doctor's prognosis. The doctor hunched at his difficult desk and projected compassion and concern. To the clown the walls of the doctor's office seemed to smoke and bubble like some molten gray Jell-O off in the distance. He scrupulously pondered the options the doctor had offered.

"Well, let's see here. These are my options. I can let them install a machine inside my lower back to emit electrical impulses that temporarily confuse the pain signals to my brain, or I can take morphine for the rest of my life," thought the clown.

He could almost hear the junkies of the world audibly drooling for Door Number Two. He also knew that morphine meant more morphine, meant more and more morphine, until there isn't enough morphine in the whole wide world and you have to kick and start over. And the kicking is painful, and the distance between kicks keeps getting tighter until you explode!

He already knew that. They didn't call him the temple of accumulated error for nothing. He already possessed the surface model of the dorsal-column stimulator suggested in option Number One. It was more nuisance than benefactor, although the concept of being even slightly bionic would

*have once amused him. No more! This clown had lost his
sense of humor. Who would have believed it? Most certainly
not the clown. He had always prided himself in his ability to
laugh at the tough stuff. No more.*

*"Gimme a couple days to think about this," he an-
swered the doctor over his shoulder. He was already out the
door and into the gray Jell-O.*

*The clown blinked twice and discovered himself back in
his own room in his own bed. He remotely remembered
writing the note and swallowing every pill in the place. "Fuck
it," he rasped and then came the blessed oblivion.*

The duration of my oblivion is debatable. In what seemed
a few murky moments, I was snatched from the infamous jaws
of death. It is common knowledge that cannibals do not eat
clowns because they taste funny. Death, however, has no such
culinary bias. Just why I was rejected is anybody's guess. The
fact remains that death bit down, found me wanting, and spat
me back into the world.

I was later informed that at the moment of my audible
re-entry, the *Berkeley Barb* was on the telephone in the hallway. They were composing a commemorative issue on the
sixties and requested my comments on that turbulent decade.
At that same moment my acupuncturist, Evon Karanoff, in-
serted a needle into my flesh that made me cry "Ouch!" They
printed it in the newspaper.

On the afternoon of my resurrection a strange letter
floated into our Woolsey Street house. It was from a woman
named Cherie who worked at a Polarity Center in Boulder
Creek. Cherie said I had appeared in a dream and she felt she
was able to cure my back through polarity. This was the straw
we were clutching at. My wife loaded me into her Datsun
wagon and boogied to Boulder Creek. I had no opinion about

anything. I merely went along for the ride. Mostly I remember her driving through puffs of swirling gray Jell-O.

My first conscious memory was of drinking the tea. It was vile, disgusting stuff composed of velarian roots and other odious bushes. I call it all "hot water on bushes."

For the first week they just poured me full of these particular bushes. "They" were Sandy, the woman who owned the house, plus Jean and Cherie, her stalwart staff. Make that double stalwart. They had to hold me down and polarize me night and day while I wrestled with withdrawal from the opiates and barbiturates of nearly a decade. I vividly recall a legion of sharp-toothed and nearly translucent snakes that hovered just over my face as I attempted to snooze.

On one occasion I was presented with a two-hundred-year-old ginseng root by the herbalist Michael Tierra. The women sliced up the root and made a tea, which they then gently forced me to drink. Whamm! This monster mega-dose of ginseng lifted me up out of Jell-O-ville and oblivion central, and elevated me to my highest human potential. It only lasted about five hours, but in that short time I was able to put my life in order and, more important, to actually feel good about myself and my potential as a future human.

After the first week I was allowed the luxury of steamed vegetables to go with my tea. I would begin each day with a bracing blast of wheatgrass juice. This stuff tasted like somebody's lawn. When I recovered from breakfast, they would gently guide me outdoors and into the sunshine, where I was anointed with either olive oil, castor oil, or the essence of vitamin E, which we procured from the local feed store at little cost.

After the second week I began to gain some weight. I had finally bottomed out at seventy-eight pounds. "There's no place like the bottom." Here I paraphrase St. Francis of Assisi, who added, "Then you can really get some momentum." With momentum came my ability for focus free of snakes and Jell-O.

The sight of my naked form in a full-length mirror came as a terrible shock. I was so skinny I had no sideways. My full frontal skin and bones would make a Nazi blush. I began to consume vast quantities of steamed vegetables and tea. After two months of twenty-four-hour tender loving care, my health angels mailed me to Boston to attend the Hypocrites Health Institute and prepare for my re-entry into the real world.

Hypocrites was the brainchild of one Ann Wigmore. She had lived on weeds and grasses while a fugitive during World War II and inadvertently discovered their healing properties. Her Boston brownstone was a testament to that teaching, as I soon discovered.

Upon entering my assigned quarters, I found my roommate reclining on a slantboard with a stiff dose of wheatgrass implanted up his butt. Laugh if you must. I must confess it blew my battered brain to see him thus inclined. Within a month's time, my silent laughter turned to awe when I accompanied him to Harvard for his follow-up X-rays. The cancer in his prostate had disappeared. The doctors were beside themselves. The only explanation offered was the wheat grass, which I then embraced whole hog.

I changed my name to H.M. (Hugh Man) Bean and began to guzzle lawns that I would plant and harvest in two-foot earthen flats. Thus I did snip each day my daily blades of grass, which I would then feed into the hand-turned grinder that made the foul emerald fluid that helped to save my life. My diet also included several species of sprout—alfalfa, sunflower, mung bean, et cetera—and a dressing of fermented sesame or sunflower seeds.

I was salvaged from this demented grazing by some deep-cover hippies on the staff who recognized me from the Woodstock film and whisked me off to their quarters for a little sensemilla and Chocolate Ice Cream.

"Where can I get some more of that shit?" I bellowed as the chocolate blasted home.

They drew me a map to the nearest health food store to which I would make illicit forays through the nighttime snow. In this manner I discovered the wonders of health food junk food, like cashew butter and wayfarer's bread, which I would consume greedily under the covers.

In fourteen years' time, this here under-the-cover clown would more than triple his girthage by industrious consumption of everything in sight.

In truth, I am aware that I was rescued from the gray lips of the grim reaper by skilled and caring humans in consort with wheatgrass, sprouts, and the terrible teas.

The next time I'm dying I'll be sure to dig in.

Meanwhile, my life rolls on, so rich and full of awesome wonder I am occasionally ashamed. Ashamed that I once said "Fuck it" and gave up.

I was resurrected to this life by the grace of fate and the angels of health. I realize I am the living goof and I practice resurrection every chance I get.

Basic Human Needs

ENTER WAVY GRAVY. Mr. Gravy is attired in the regalia of the political clown. He is wearing (from the top down) his nearly trademark battered black derby, which neatly crowns his graying wavy bozo locks. His face is coated in flat clown white pancake makeup. Mr. Gravy employs the generous red mouth and nose of the traditional clown. Sometimes he places a large red nose over his already existing olfactory organ. This addition squeeks when it is squozen. His beady blue eyes are surrounded by twin rainbows of clown paint that also match his ruff. His jumpsuit is constructed from the fields of forty flags. It contains all the stars and none of the bars. Giant blue-and-white 1942 wingtip shoes complete the ensemble . . . I almost forgot the giant black-and-white peace sign pinned over his heart. Around the insignia is printed the slogan BACK BY POPULAR DEMAND. In his right hand he is clutching a bizarre one-stringed instrument from India, which he begins to pluck as he approaches the microphone. Wavy is joined on stage by three winsome tie-dyed maidens the program identifies as . . . The Wavettes.

WAVY: "Years and years of driving around in these crazy painted buses and we'd drive up to somebody who was far out and we'd say, 'Hey, where's it at?' And they would give us their version; and we kept stacking up these various versions . . . like if you stick a candle between two mirrors, you get this arc of lights that stretches to infinity and this song is that arc of lights. As I said to the mirror the other morning, it's all done with people.''

(He begins to sing the verses and is joined on each chorus by Wavettes.)

BASIC HUMAN NEEDS

A Song for One String
by Wavy Gravy

Wouldn't it be neat
If the people that you meet
had shoes upon their feet
and something to eat?

And wouldn't it be fine
if all humankind
had shelter.

(Chorus)
Basic Human Needs
Basic Human Deeds
Doin' What Comes Naturally.
Down in the Garden
Where No One Is Apart
Deep Down in the Garden
The Garden of Your Heart.

Wouldn't it be grand
if we all lent a hand
so each one could stand
on a free piece of land?

And wouldn't it be thrilling
if folks stopped their killing
and started in tilling the land?

(Chorus)

Not just churches,
not just steeples,
give me people helping people.

Help yourself and work out
till the stars begin to shout
thank god for something to do.

(Chorus)

What a great day it would be
if everyone could see
and no one was blind unnecessarily
cuz it's hard yes, it's hard to be blind
(and disabled . . . basic human needs).

(Chorus)

Wouldn't it be fun
if the shine down from the sun
could power everyone?
And uranium slept forever in the ground.

(Chorus)

Wouldn't it be daring
if folks started sharing
instead of comparing
what each other was wearing?

And wouldn't it be swell
if people didn't sell their mother
Earth.

(Chorus)

CUT TO WAVY GRAVY AT HOME. Mr. Gravy is now casu-
ally attired and his pink and portly face is finally free of clown
makeup.

WAVY: "Basic Human Needs" is the best song I ever
wrote. Which isn't saying much; I've only written three songs
in my entire life. "Harpo's Ladder," which is my silly clown
anthem singalong, ends up with the audience putting bags over
their heads and doing the farting noises I call the Funny Mantra.
"Harpo's Ladder" is the ultimate ice-breaker.
"Take Whatever You Need to Be You" is the world's
shortest love song. I recorded it in 1973 with Jeremy Steig and
Eddie Gomez for Just Sunshine Records. They also recorded
"Basic Human Needs" with Maria Muldaur swapping lead vo-
cals with me and her Midnight at the Oasis band. Those cuts
were never released. The project was nixed by Big Tony from
the upper echelon of Just Sunshine's parent company, Gulf +
Western. Big Tony said, "Tell him we don't want to save the
earth. We want to save the vinyl!"
It took almost fifteen years for my tunes to go into popular
release. They are now available on Relix Records with Maria's
daughter Jenny joining Wavettes Susy Barsotti and Jahanara.
The album is called Wavy Gravy, the 80's Are the 60's Twenty
Years Later: Old Feathers New Bird. Basic Human Needs was
recorded off the board of the Berkeley Community Theater on
the occasion of my fiftieth birthday benefit by Jay Yarnell and
Richard Sales of Glass Wing Records. Richard mixed in the

synthesizers in his Baltimore studio and sold the package to Les Kippel at Relix.

By that time I knew my song well. Real well. I don't know about it being "my" song, though. The darn thing just sort of reared up and wrote itself in a couple of hours.

DISSOLVE TO: Interior shot of Wavy, alone in a small shingled dome in the Santa Cruz mountains. He is scribbling madly in the back of a large looseleaf phone book. The year is 1971.

CAMERA PAN FROM OVER GRAVY'S SHOULDER TO CLOSE-UP ON THE PAGE. WE SEE HIM SCRIBBLE, "Wouldn't it be neat . . . His gaunt frame barely fills the faded forty-year-old hippie T-shirt. His eyes smolder like old cigarettes in their sunken sockets.

Look carefully through those windows of the soul, Ladies and Gentlemen. His shades are drawn. Although his hand is writing the song, his mind is having a noon meal at that cafeteria of the clouds. That man is in no condition to write his own name, let alone a song like "Basic Human Needs." Yet his quivering hand continues to add verse after verse.

Yet he is not writing it.

But if not him . . . who? Or if not who, what?

What is the force that continues to write during Mr. Gravy's mental lunch break? It is nothing more or less than the juice of the muse. The invisible, unnamable flow that has produced intuitive creation through history. Like any honest author, I must hereby acknowledge that I am only a willing accomplice in the unending universal conspiracy of living letters . . .

Dead Center

Somewhere in my stuff I have this realistic life-sized rubber skull mask. An instant Deadhead, which I save for special occasions . . . like the Death and Dying Camp that Ram Dass ran with Stephan Levine in Yucca Valley.

Ram Dass is an ex-Harvard psychology professor who dropped out of academia and went to India, where he met his guru and changed his name from Richard Alpert to Ram Dass. His guru's name was Maharaji or the Neem Karoli Baba. Maharaji has already left his body but his spirit and photos are everywhere I go. He looks a whole lot like Popeye in a plaid blanket. As I learn more about his great heart and impish sense of humor I feel he is my kinda guru.

So is Ram Dass, who claims to be Nobody's guru. Now I can relate to that cuz I'm Nobody's fool. In fact, when we were running Nobody for president in 1984 we were campaigning in the New Hampshire primary. Ram Dass showed up at our rally and asked what could he do to help. I sat him down at this little card table with the simple instructions, ''The bumper stickers are a dollar and the buttons are fifty cents.'' I think the Maharaji made me do it!

So I was truly honored to assist R.D. in his Yucca Valley experiment. Stephan Levine and I have a long and checkered history together going back beyond our days of beatnik glory in Greenwich Village all the way to Albany, New York, in the forties, when we both attended P.S. 16. Stephan was and is a really great poet who also ran the Dying Project in New Mexico for Ram Dass and the Hanuman Foundation.

Hanuman is the Hindu monkey god and perfect servant of Ram, who is God. Some people don't know that and call Ram Dass "Ram," which is really hilarious and undoubtedly part of Popeye's great plan. The addition of Dass, which means servant, brings the whole thing into a less pretentious perspective.

He and Stephan have served as pioneers in the great work of using death as a springboard for spiritual awakening. Attending their workshop were hospice workers and the dying, along with those who had recently lost a loved one; and me!

I had just put in a lot of years mapping unfamiliar trenches as the clown in residence at the Oakland Children's Hospital. The prospect of unloading some of my more brutal baggage among colleagues was heaven-sent.

The venue was the Institute of Mentalphysics in Yucca Valley, where I had met my own personal teacher a decade before. His name was Edwin J. Dingle. He wore a gold suit and was over a hundred and twenty years old. It was a glorious Easter Sunday afternoon when my wife and I poured out of the Joshua Tree National Monument. After some high-altitude sunrise shenanigans, we coasted downhill into Yucca Valley. I noticed this little village made of triangles and pulled into the parking lot for a better peek.

Inside the main sanctuary an Easter service was in progress. Mr. Dingle, known affectionately to his followers as Ding La Mei, was shouting, "The Truth!" from the pulpit and lotused behind him was a younger man. This was the Reverend Donald Walthrop, who slightly resembled Dr. Strange. In fact, I could see a blue beam of energy pass from out of Walthrop into Dingle and then out into the congregation, who pushed it through the roof!

I was really impressed! I kept the Easter program and signed up for weekly classes in Los Angeles.

Every Wednesday evening I would gather with a covey of blue-haired little old ladies and several Jamaican dishwashers. We would sit in this musky old room with red light bulbs and listen enraptured to Mr. Dingle speaking on the tape recorder.

"This is the voice of Edwin J. Dingle . . ." and then he would reveal little nuggets of Buddhism enmeshed in a rich broth of mystic Christianity, but mainly he taught these breaths, which he allegedly learned fifty years before in a lamasery in Tibet.

At that time he was a cartographer mapping the Himalayas. He was caught in a storm and sought refuge amid the monks. In time they would teach him these amazing breaths, which he passed on to us via tape and text.

I would take them home and practice every morning, with interesting results. So much so, the Dingle breaths are still very much a part of my spiritual practices.

It was a righteous rush to return to the scene of my earliest efforts at actualization. Reverend Dingle had long since shuffled off his mortal coil, while Donald Walthrop is still in attendance as a kinda cosmic caretaker. He still remembered me after all these years and said I was a really good breather.

Flushed with pride, I unpacked my hats and noses, giant shades and shoes, bubbles and assorted clown *puja,* dusted off my rubber death's-head skull, and set out to hook up with the rest of my fellow campers in the mass meeting hall adjacent to the sanctuary.

There we would gather each morning for lectures by Stephan and R.D., interspersed with hands-on exercises, chanting meditations. The main technique taught was Vapasanna breathing.

This practice involves sitting with a straight back and

watching your breath. Every time your mind wanders, gently bring your focus back to the breath. Breathing In . . . (One hundred and twenty of us all on the same breath) . . . Breathing Out . . . (After ten minutes of this, I enter a somewhat altered state) . . . Breathing In . . . (The walls are breathing with us) . . . Breathing Out . . . (Altered state my ass, we are experiencing a major Earthquake) . . . Breathing In (Everybody does so, except for this one woman who leaps up and flies to Pennsylvania just in time for Three Mile Island. The rest of us simply surrendered) . . . Breathing Out (and lived happily ever after . . . at least for the rest of the afternoon).

Later in the day I ran a field trip into the epicenter of the ex-earthquake called "Dangerous Adventures with Wavy Gravy." I expected a herd of adrenaline junkies but encountered several vanloads of terrified fellow humans seeking an opportunity to eat up their fear of earthquakes.

We drove into the Joshua Tree Monument and proceeded to climb Skull Rock blindfolded (with peeking optional). The adventure was both a breakthrough and big fun. I got to wear my rubber skull head for the first time in public. The addition of my giant sunglasses successfully smashed the face of Mr. Death and almost made it funny.

I've always maintained death is Patrick Henry's second choice . . . and nature's way of telling us to *slow down*. I seriously honor death as the great liberator with terrible press. In my work at the Children's Hospital I recommend the book *Life After Life,* by Dr. Raymond Moody, to the parents. This is a collection of interviews from people pronounced clinically dead and then brought back to life. Not one of them remotely suggested that death sucked. *Au contraire,* they really enjoyed the death process and were somewhat miffed at their return to sentient status.

The kids were always cool as they have no heavy preconceptions on the subject. Encouraged by a suggestion of Elisabeth Kübler-Ross, I would have the children that I worked with do paintings and drawings of where they would go when they died. The friendly vistas of their imaginations were filled with bluebirds, rainbows, and dear departed relatives. My advice to the kids has remained constant over the years . . . "When it feels right, just drop your body like some old rags and keep moving toward the light."

The days at camp danced by in a beatific blur of people sharing together, absorbing each other's pain and anguish in the clean fresh light of the moment. One evening I got to introduce the gun game, which originated somewhere in the pre-history of improvisational theater. The rules are simple. All players possessed an invisible gun and three imaginary shots. We used Day-Glo sticky paper dots for bullets. When you shot someone, they had to die the most dramatic death they could conceive of at that given moment. Upon resurrection they would mount their assailant's Day-Glo dot on their own forehead. Three dots and you were immortal and out of the game. Conscientious objectors could stick on their own dots and be done with it. Oh yes, no shooting anyone doing a job or carrying hot or fragile stuff.

Well, the shoot-em-up was going great guns with deaths and resurrections all over the meeting-room floor when this sweet old lady started to freak out! I think her name was Polly. She was well into her eighties, confined to a wheelchair, and suffered horribly from Alzheimer's disease.

"Bring me Ram Dass," she gasped.

He arrived posthaste and knelt by her chair . . . the whole hall held its collective breath. Polly spastically raised her afghan shawl to reveal a palsied hand holding her invisible 45 magnum.

"Bang! said Polly as she drilled the astonished Mr. Dass

with a Day-Glo dum-dum, and successfully opened his third eye. His demise and subsequent resurrection were both inspired and anti-climactic.

I'll close this piece with the parable of the man who runs up to the zen master and asks, "What happens when I die?"

"How do I know?" inquired the zen master.

"Well, you're a zen master!"

"Yeah, but not a dead one."

Sigh Along with Mitch

Mitch Snyder was the patron saint of the homeless and disenfranchised in America. His public fast to near-death caused the Reagan administration to release a viable structure to the homeless community of Washington, D.C. Mitch helped forge it into the largest and best-equipped habitat for homeless on the planet.

Mitch Snyder had iron eyes, curly brown hair, and a scruffy Kurt Vonnegut moustache that fringed his stern mouth. Martin Sheen played him in a television docudrama, but in real life Mitch Snyder played very little.

He had a no-nonsense way of getting stuff done. Lots of stuff.

It took all my guile and cunning as a spontaneous clown to solicit as much as a smile out of Snyder. I took it on as a major challenge and sometimes was rewarded with a hard-won chortle or guffaw.

I went to jail with Mitch in the fall of '88. I was in D.C. with the Vicious Hippies (a rock-and-roll band) and the Nobody for President campaign.

Mitch had planned an act of civil disobedience to dramatize the plight of the homeless. So after our Nobody rally across the street from the White House, I streaked straight to Constitution Avenue, where all the homeless advocates were being arrested. They were being systematically handcuffed and loaded onto buses, then driven off to holding pens for photos and fingerprinting.

I was once again tardy for my bust, but after being put briefly on hold by a high-ranking fuzz, I was allowed to exercise my constitutional rights; i.e., get arrested.

It was a great thrill for me to be popped with the likes of Mitch Snyder and Dr. Benjamin Spock. My arresting officer was so preoccupied with my clown apparel that he was somewhat slipshod in his application of my plastic handcuffs. On the bus to the joint I was able to slip free and start blowing bubbles. The bus driver was beside himself with rage because he couldn't ascertain the origin of the bubbles, and I wasn't about to bust myself.

Mitch had a good laugh when he got wind of that one. It made me feel awfully good to make Mitch laugh. He asked me to help get talent for a rally to be held following the great homeless march on Washington held the following year. I was to work closely with Bill Graham, who was the main organizer. Graham is the Sol Hurok of rock-and-roll, and it was a real delight for me to work with him on such a pure and righteous cause. It must have been extremely eerie for artists to get us both on their respective cases, as we have extremely different techniques of doing business—or in this case, charity.

Every couple of days I would call up Bill and bug him about our commitment to come through for Mitch. "Bill," I would pester, "we gotta get some acts. Mitch is not eating till we get some good acts."

Bill never let on if he knew whether I was kidding or not, but boy, did we get some acts. Stevie Wonder, Dionne Warwick, Tracy Chapman, the Jefferson Airplane, and Los Lobos

come immediately to mind. We had Jesse Jackson, Dick Greg-
ory, Martin Sheen, Coretta Scott King, Jon Voight, Susan
Sarandon, and Valerie Harper among the list of speakers.

I got to start that day marching in a parade with Sugar Ray
Leonard and a couple hundred schoolchildren. These kids were
pulling little red wagons full of letters from schoolkids all over
America and addressed to the president of the United States.
Letters asking him to please help the homeless.

That afternoon I got to introduce the Jefferson Airplane,
who played my all-time favorite sixties anthem, "Volunteers of
America," to this sea of swirling hippies, straights, and hopeful
homeless. Hopeful because advocates from everywhere joined
them in their dancing. Dancing in the shadow of the Capitol
dome.

The show had a beautiful shape to it and I kept watching
it build and build throughout the afternoon. Starting with
Mickey Hart and Ollatunji, and winding all the way through the
day, winding down with Warwick and Wonder. The speeches
and the music intertwined with sunshine and a sense of caring
rubbed off onto the bused-in thousands as they bathed in the
knowledge that they were not alone.

Backstage was as snug and mellow as I've ever seen it.
Here was big lumbering Lou Gossett, Jr., sucking in his gut to
slip by Coretta Scott King, who is headed for the hospitality
tent. And just who is that *clown* doing backstage security—by
the ramp leading up to the stage?

I couldn't help but deputize myself to regulate the ebb and
flow of legends up and down the ramp. If they got by me they
had to deal with Bill Graham and the Barsotti brothers, who
were stationed stage right.

Mitch got a real kick out of watching me doing my rock-
and-roll clown cop. In fact that whole day was one giant
affirmation for Mitch Snyder and the whole homeless move-

ment. . . . or so it seemed on the surface. The more complex reality was that Housing Now! took a tremendous toll on both Mitch and his companion, Carol Finley. In fact after the show they were both burned to a crisp. Although the rally was the lead story on all national and local media reports, the turnout for the march was much smaller than the half million they had anticipated the year before. Also a major rift went down between the planners and some of the marchers.

Wasted and discouraged, Carol took a break but somehow Mitch kept working. He told Carol he was "too tired to go on and too committed to quit."

Six months later Mitch Snyder hung himself. He did it on the third day of July, in the year of Our Lord, nineteen hundred and ninety. As I type this piece, the one-year anniversary of Mitch's death is almost upon us. After the ice-cold splash of horror dries off, I think we all try desperately to fill up that black and empty vacuum that inevitably occurs. With the benefit of hindsight we search to make sense of the senseless.

Personally, I kept kicking myself for not checking in with Mitch from time to time with a simple dose of humor on the phone. When I called Carol at the Center for Non-Violent Study, she helped to put my guilt to rest. Carol said if any lesson was to be learned from Mitch it should be from his life and not his death. She said he did not die as an excuse for the people in the movement to fear a similar burnout and take more vacations. I am paraphrasing here but I think her parting words to me were, "Don't *ever* slow down."

To which I parried, "Dare to struggle, dare to grin!"

Her ensuing laughter was an awful lot like Mitch's.

A Quick Sketch of My Thumbnail

Dear Reader:

You have more Gravy on your eyes. My favorite introduction occurred at the United Nations, when I was presented to the press corps as Wavy Gravy, humanitarian, activist, and ah . . . ahhh . . . ah—clown!

Here is a quick sketch of my thumbnail.

Born: Hugh Romney, May 15, 1936, East Greenbush, New York.

Sign: Slippery when wet.

Education: P.S. 16, Albany, New York. William Hall High School, West Hartford, Connecticut. Volunteered for the military draft in the fall of '54 and was honorably discharged after twenty-two months of service in the United States Army. (I am in no way recommending the military as a career choice. The Korean War had just wound down and I figured it was a reasonable assumption that I could slip in and out before the next little war rolled around. It was a dumb decision on my part but it helped pay for my college education.)

1957: Entered Boston University Theater Department under the Korean G.I. Bill. Started jazz and poetry on the east coast at Pat's Pebble in the Rock on Huntington Avenue in Boston. After a year and a half, defected to the Neighborhood Playhouse School of the Theater in New York City. Graduated in 1961.

1958–1962: Attended Neighborhood Playhouse by day, served by night as poetry and entertainment director (with John Brent) at the Gaslight Café in Greenwich Village. (I went from being a published teen-aged beatnik poet to hip comic tongue dancer right before my very eyes.) Was married to Elizabeth by a Blind Harlem street singer and preacher named Reverend Gary Davis in the Gaslight.

1962: Moved to California at the request of Lenny Bruce, who became my part-time manager. Recorded "Hugh Romney, Third Stream Humor" for World Pacific Records. (I recorded this live when I was the opening act for Thelonious Monk on the night the great Club Renaissance closed its doors forever.)

1963: Joined the Committee, an improvisational theater company in San Francisco. Daughter Sabrina born. Purchased a condo in Marin City and a Packard Caribbean convertible in Hollywood. Tuned in, turned on, and dropped out—way out. Entered deep space. Left wife, daughter, and stuff and journeyed to northern Arizona to join up with Hopi Indians and await the coming global cataclysm. (The Hopis said I was early but let me hang out anyway and regroup my head.) Connected with interconnectedness of everything and surrendered to Law of Sacred Coincidence.

Returned to Los Angeles and regrouped life. Divorced wife, gave away stuff, and began to float aimlessly on the ocean of one thing after another.

1964: Financed free-floating lifestyle through sale of single ounces of marijuana packaged in decorator bags and containing tiny toys. (The dubious apex of this short-lived profession was when I scored a kilo for the Beatles.) Met Bonnie Jean Beecher at her restaurant, the Fred C. Dobbs. She put peanuts in my hamburger. Together we survived. L.A. Acid Tests and in 1965 we married each other. We also married the Hog Farm. The Hog Farm is the name still associated with our expanded family. We acquired it while living rent free on a mountaintop in Sunland, California, in exchange for the caretaking of forty actual hogs. Within a year of moving there, the people engaged in our bizarre communal experiment began to outnumber the pigs. At first we all had separate jobs. I had a grant to teach brain-damaged children improvisation while teaching a similar class to contract players at Columbia Pictures. Harrison Ford was one of my students. My wife Bonnie was a successful television actress. Joining the scene were musicians, a computer programmer, a race-car driver, a telephone company executive, a cinematographer, several mechanics, and a heap of hippies.

1966: We performed light shows and energy games at the Shrine Exposition Hall in Los Angeles with Cream, Jimi Hendrix, the Jefferson Airplane, and the Grateful Dead. The Shrine holds ten thousand people. On Sunday afternoons we had free happenings on our mountaintop. Maybe a hundred people in open celebration.

1967: We scored a couple of old school buses with funds earned as extras in Otto Preminger's movie, *Skidoo*, and outfitted them for our exodus. I underwent my first spinal surgery and joined the caravan of Hog Farmers in New Mexico.

1968: Summer Solstice. Accompanying our extensive entourage was Pigasus Pig, the first female black-and-white hog-candidate for president. We debuted our traveling road show at the Los Alamos proving grounds and set off cross-country to share our open celebration with the rest of the free world. *(Driver! The United States of America! And step on it!)* We were a light show, a rock band, a painting, a poem, an anti-war rally, an anthem for freedom and change. Mostly we were a palette for the audience to blast off from, and the audience was also the spaceship and the star. Bought twelve-acre farm in Llano, New Mexico.

1969: Served as chief of the Please Force at the Woodstock music festival, where the Hog Farm administered the free kitchen and bad-trip/freak-out tent. Was captured in the movie "Woodstock" and propelled into the world press. Became good-humored peacemaker and purveyor of life support at major rock festivals and political demonstrations of the sixties and seventies. Changed name to Wavy Gravy at the Texas Pop Festival. Experienced spinal fusion and acquired all-star cast.

1970: Helped initiate an experiment of buying back the earth and deeding it back to itself. Purchased 590 acres in northern Vermont and called it Earth People's Park. Made a movie, *Medicine Ball Caravan,* for Warner Brothers, which ended up in England.

1971: Journeyed with two buses filled with food, medical supplies, and forty-two people from seventeen countries, to Pakistan and the Himalayas. Returned to United States and captured record for having the largest number of active diseases in a single human being at Roosevelt Hospital in New York City. Upon my release, I dictated my book *The Hog Farm and Friends* and traveled to the west coast.

1972: Third and final spinal fusion. The surgery left me in my cast of thousands, firmly ensconced at Pacific High School in the Santa Cruz mountains. This is a center for alternative education rented by David Crosby for me to recuperate at with the whole Hog Farm. Bonnie Jean gave birth to Howdy Do-Good Gravy at the Tomahawk Truckstop in Boulder, Colorado. We helped the Zippies run a rock for president and a roll for vice president (so you can always eat the vice president); I lose the rock in a New York taxicab. We traveled to Sweden for the United Nations Conference on Human Environment with a contingent of eco-freaks, indigenous Americans, poets, scientists, and Margaret Mead.

1973: Blanko.

1974: The largest teaching hospital in Southeast Asia was destroyed by U.S. bombers on Christmas Day. I joined others in effort to rebuild Bach Mai hospital. Camp Winnarainbow founded in the Mendocino woodlands.

1975: Woolsey Street house purchased by the Hog Farm, followed soon thereafter by the founding of the Babylon Telephone Answering Service on the front porch. I attended World Survival Symposium in Chapel Hill, North Carolina, and started a new world religion in San Francisco called The First Church of Fun. Wife Bonnie Jean takes Sufi name, "Jahanara."

1976: American bicentennial and birth of the Birthday Party, which nominated Nobody for president. I journeyed to Kansas and the Republican convention, where I was advised by state and federal agents, "Get out of here. You're too weird to arrest." Tenth wedding anniversary. Bill Graham produces *The Last Waltz*. I told him, "Bill, you shouldn't have."

1977: More blanko.

1978: Temporarily died in Berkeley and was later resurrected in Boulder Creek and Boston.

1979: Purchased the Henry Street house and sold Woolsey Street house, with the exception of the front porch, where we continued to maintain our answering service. The Seva Foundation founded in Heartlands, Michigan.

1980: "Nobody for President" tours cross-country in the family Greyhound, which is temporarily dubbed "The Nobody One."

1982: Began purchase of land in Laytonville, California, called Black Oak Ranch.

1983: Moved Camp Winnarainbow to Laytonville.

1984: Toured in Greyhound bus with Unreal Band for Nobody. Seva "Sing Out for Sight" concert held outside Toronto with The Band and the Grateful Dead.

1986: Turn fifty. Had mind blown publicly by family and friends at massive Berkeley benefit.

1987: Jerry Garcia, with acoustic and electric bands, inaugurated our annual fundraiser to help pay for Black Oak Ranch. Produced in cahoots with Bill Graham, it is called "Electric on the Eel."

1988: Nobody IV tour, with the rock band Vicious Hippies. We went from sea to shining sea. Busted with the homeless in Washington, D.C. Help produce Home Aid Concert for The Seva Foundation in New York City at the Cathedral of St. John the Divine.

1989: Woodstock twenty-year anniversary.

1990: Hog Farm twenty-five-year reunion. Ran for Berkeley City Council with slogan "Let's elect a real clown for a change." Lost election, but kept marbles, mind, mittens, and sense of humor.

1992: Became ice-cream flavor for Ben & Jerry's.

Early Einstein

Folks are constantly badgering me to dredge up my very early years. I usually tell them my chromosomes have amnesia, which is always good for a chuckle and a change of subject, but it doesn't always work.

What people really want to know about is Albert Einstein. Rumor is, he took me for walks when I was five years old and living in Princeton, New Jersey. It's true.

Our apartment was situated right in the good professor's flight plan, with me behind a white picket fence in the front yard for my afternoon airing. The connection was kismet because: a) I was as cute as a button (Wilke Dewey—no, better make that Churchill. Most well-fed toddlers resemble Winston Churchill); and b) Einstein was looking for company. Maybe he needed someone to bounce his ideas off without fear of rebuttal.

My mom's flabber was properly gasted when her firstborn male child was out walking with Einstein. I'm sure I was thoroughly debriefed after each outing.

Now it's fifty years down the block and I don't remember much.

I do recall the white-haired explosion on Albert's head that predated Don King by nearly half a century. I do remember his two-eyed twinkle, below which bristled his marvelous moustache. The gray sweatshirt (no logo) and sneakers (ditto) are still clear in my mind. Most of all I remember his smile and his *smell*.

I refer to an odor that resembles nothing my nostrils have ever encountered from earliest childhood until this present date. I'll just keep on sniffin' my way through life and someday, somewhere, I'm gonna shout out, "Hey, Buddy, you smell just like Albert Einstein."

My memories of that era evoke mainly Mason Riggin, the boy next door. Mason was chronologically five years old but was pushing the edge of the teenage envelope in his sense of daring and exploration. I desperately envied his classy cowboy costume, with matching pearl-handled cap pistols and a bottomless Hopalong Cassidy lunch bucket.

I was Mason Riggin's faithful flunky. Every Saturday afternoon we would go to the movies together. It was always a double feature plus five cartoons, a newsreel, maybe a travelog, a serial, and previews of coming attractions. After eyeballing a couple of horse operas we sashayed back to our secret corral in the woods behind Mason's house.

He was determined to re-create what we witnessed that day on the silver screen, namely, a good old-fashioned hanging starring him and his mother's clothesline. Mason made himself up a nifty little noose and tossed it over an obliging tree limb. Next, he climbed bravely up on a battered old soapbox, clipped that noose around his neck and requested that I "kick the soap box out from under me, and get on with the hanging!" Which I did forthwith.

Well, you should have seen old Mason thrashing and crashing about, just like in the movies, only better. Instead of black and white, Mason Riggin was in barely living, livid color. His head had turned a bright and basic blue. His ankles were twitching spastically when I freaked out and ran to fetch his father.

Mr. Riggin came a runnin' on the double, and cut down his kid in the nick of time. Mason gurgled for breath as his blue head turned briefly red and then back to a justly terrified shade of pink.

However, in the process of his son's rescue, Mr. Riggin had stumbled into our secret shitter. To this day I can see him floundering in his spiffy Florsheims, up to his argyles in our childhood feces. Mr. Riggin's head turned beet red as he swiftly stomped to safety with his resurrected son firmly in tow. No sooner did Mason begin breathing again than his old man began walloping him on the behind.

Wham!!!

"That'll teach you to use a proper toilet."

Wham!!!

From behind the hanging tree I watched in horror and fascination as the painful lesson was pounded home.

And so it was in the first of the forties that I learned that $E = MC^2$ and to always bury my shit. When my own son, Howdy Do-good, was born I was determined that his first intelligent utterance should be Einstein's theory of relativity. Alas, he never got past the Eeeeee.

Oh well, it's the biggest letter on the eye chart. I may have to settle for an optometrist.

Bye Bye Bill

I knew the moment Janahara opened the bedroom door. Dazed and half-asleep, I knew in an instant of brilliant clarity that someone had died. I girded my psyche and slipped into overdrive. I was fifty-five years old and people were starting to die of natural causes; we had just buried my beloved brother-in-law Brook Beecher in the family plot up north. I jumped up, wide awake, and thought I was ready for anything.

When my wife whispered that Bill Graham had been killed in a helicopter crash I lost it. Bill Graham dead? It didn't compute. I always believed he was invincible, that somehow he would kick Death's ass.

"Yo, Death! Outta here!"

. . . and Death would sheepishly shuffle off in quest of more meek and mortal fare.

I turned on the television and switched to CNN, where the impossible imposed itself upon the cathode. Bill's demise seemed to be big news. The CNN announcer described the high winds and heavy rains that caused Bill's helicopter to crash into an electrical tower. An image of the wrecked helicopter wedged intractably into the side of the tower burned into my brain as the disembodied voice of the announcer droned on.

"All parties were instantly electrocuted. Bill Graham, his pilot and friend Steve 'Killer' Kahn, and close companion Melissa Gold. At the moment of impact several nearby towns were left without power."

The date was October 25, 1991. Bill Graham was sixty years old.

I had known him for nearly half of those years. Our relationship began with the Winterlands and the Fillmores of yesteryear, where he wet-nursed the infant Rock-and-Roll for our amusement, and for our money. He caught a tremendous amount of shit for daring to make a profit, and many of my close friends thought of Bill as an enemy who was ripping off the culture. I always thought that was bullshit and found myself in the slightly uncomfortable position of defending Bill to the movement. Sure, at first glance he appeared to be an unashamed hustler with a seething temper. His bursts of rage were legendery but he never, ever hustled the audience. He always provided a great show at a fair price, and with each production upgraded something: better lights, better sound, cleaner restrooms. In time, Bill Graham and his fledgling company Bill Graham Presents became masters of public assemblage and performance. His international tours for supergroups like the Rolling Stones were run with Swiss precision and order.

He produced a million benefits, and vowed each one would be his last: Live Aid, the Amnesty tour, the Concert Against AIDS. The list goes on and on. I worked with Bill on several of these shows and felt our friendship deepen into love and almost family.

In the last five years, I witnessed an amazing metamorphosis in Bill. He hollered at people less. The acts of love and kindness—which he hid for years behind a gruff exterior—became more obvious and unabashed. Bill Graham mellowed. He focused less on turning the biggest profit and more on improving the human condition. When he died, he was working simultaneously on a major concert to aid the victims of the Oakland/Berkeley fire, and a summer spectacular on behalf of

Native American causes. He was beginning to glow a little around the edges.

Now he was dead and I blubbered away as I clicked desperately from channel to channel. They all carry the story now. Our phone was ringing off the hook. Nobody was ready for this, especially me. My rational mind had turned to jelly, so my subconscious swooped to the rescue:

You see, they got all these fiesty rock-and-rollers up in heaven and it's getting out of hand. St. Peter simply cannot communicate with the likes of Stevie Ray Vaughan, so they sent for Bill to create a little order. He's up there checking laminates.

I spinned this fantasy to friends and family and it helped.

This afternoon we were scheduled to assist with a Halloween party for all the foster children of Alameda County, and I was responsible for the Hog Farm face-painting team. We rolled up our sleeves and dissolved into the children. This was so therapeutic that by the time I had painted my fifteenth teenage mutant ninja turtle, I had a better grip on my grief.

The funeral was held in an opulent synagogue off the park. It was a private affair for family and friends . . . just five hundred of us crammed tastefully into a magnificent house of worship to say good-bye.

The service began with the Beatles song "Here Comes the Sun," and a rainbow of color poured through the stained-glass windows. Paul Kanter's opening remarks made us laugh: "If Bill Graham could see all these important people gathered here to say nice things about him, he would have a real good laugh." Throughout the morning, the tributes moved us back and forth between laughter and tears. Santana said it most eloquently with his instrumental solo "I Love You So Much It Hurts Me." The rabbi gave his benediction and we repaired to the sunshine and the street. Golden Gate Park glistened with the first rain of fall.

The next day began a four-day run at the Oakland Coliseum with one of Bill's favorite bands, the Grateful Dead. God forbid we should ever cancel the show—Bill had taught us that much.

Everyone shared stories about Bill. My personal favorite story took place at the Us Festival. The Kinks were due on stage but were stalling for a more favorable time slot. Bill, simply and elegantly, picked up their manager's Mercedes with a forklift and held it over the lake until the band wisely took the stage.

Once, in the Soviet Union, he threatened to cancel an entire rock festival until the Soviet generals ordered their troops to move from the front of the stage and make room for the regular fans. He also created the finest restaurant in the Soviet Union for his crew, and he denied the generals access later when they failed to possess the necessary laminates. I loved the concept of Bill going head to head with a phalanx of Soviet generals.

The following night at the Grateful Dead show in Oakland, I donned a jacket and cap printed with a map of the world. Naturally, I decided to paint my face with a road map of the Bay Area. I began to earn my keep as a spiritual clown in training by seeking out everyone I knew in need of a good laugh (which included most of Bill Graham Presents and the Grateful Dead) and presenting them with my illustrated visage. I asked them if they could find their home on my face, then I would flash the Bay Bridge, none other than my rainbow choppers. Healing holy belly laughs were pealing out left and right when Brian Auger suggested I start charging a toll. I instantly agreed because it felt so right and Bill Graham would have appreciated it. I collected about thirty-five dollars and was feeling kinda smug when I heard Bill shouting inside my head, "You shmuck, you shoulda charged the fare for the Golden Gate!'' (The Bay Bridge costs one dollar, and the Golden Gate, less than half the distance, is three times that.)

As Bill would say, ''It's not the money . . . *it's the money!*''

With the Halloween shows safely under our belt, three hundred thousand of us returned to Golden Gate Park for one final farewell to Bill, Steve, and Melissa. We trudged to the Polo Fields, the spot where I had last seen Bill. A few short weeks before, he had staged the Ben and Jerry ''One World, One Heart Festival'' which introduced my ice-cream flavor to the west coast. This Sunday was slightly more solemn.

Bobby McFerrin started off with a rendition of the Star-Spangled Banner à la Jimi Hendrix, and was followed by a galaxy of the finest musicians on the planet: Los Lobos, Santana, Jackson Browne, Journey, Joan Baez, John Fogerty, the Grateful Dead, Crosby, Stills, Nash, and Young, and on and on into the dusk.

The Hog Farm was in charge of lost children and garbage. Throughout the afternoon, I implored the audience to ''pick up a bag for Bill,'' as Hog Farmers circulated the trash bags to the multitudes. By nightfall, the meadow was spotless. Everything had been collected down to the cigarette filters. Aluminum was recycled by the homeless.

Bill would have been proud. Over three hundred thousand people had gathered together for some very good grief.

We're going to miss you, Bill. Our ears already ache for the rumble of your familiar thunder. Who else could make the lightning dance between our heartbeats? We're going to miss you . . . bad.

Always Put Your Good Where It Will Do the Most

"Always put your good where it will do the most" is a line I culled from Kesey. Ken Kesey, that is, the author of *One Flew Over the Cuckoo's Nest*. Remember that movie with Jack Nicholson? Well, before it was a movie it was a book. A great book. Even all the book critics agreed it was a great book.

So was *Sometimes a Great Notion*, which was Kesey's second book and starred Henry Fonda and Paul Newman, the guy on the salad dressing.

Forget Paul Newman for the moment. Let's stay with Kesey. He used to say one of the great secrets of life is "sticking with it," whatever "it" happens to be. He also said, "I'd rather be a lightning rod than a seismograph." Then he took this big pile of money that he made off the books and the movies and bought this funky old schoolbus. He spent a bundle fixing it up with beds and electronic gear like tape recorders and microphones and movie cameras. It filled up with his friends and they all drove off in quest of white lightning and the holy grail.

The lightning was in the punch, and quest for the grail was serialized by Tom Wolfe in *The Electric Kool-Aid Acid Test*, which will someday be a motion picture with a soundtrack by the Grateful Dead, but without Nicholson. Kesey will most likely play himself in the role of the psychedelic American superhero. He once told me, "The trouble with the superhero is what to do between phone booths." I'm still wrestling with that one.

He also said "Silence has muscles," and I'm still listening.

In *The Last Supplement to the Whole Earth Catalogue,* which Ken co-edited with Paul Krassner, he said, "Honor your father and your mother," which I suspect he lifted from a higher source. No matter. That simple quote really lit up the page for me. I immediately got on the phone and called up my parents. I told them both how much I loved and appreciated them. This really blew their minds. I mean this in a truly beautiful way.

I then called up Kesey to thank him for the hot tip. He sounded almost embarrassed. "It's just so darn simple," he said.

Most of life's lessons are just as basic. "But they only work if you work," says Wavy Gravy, slightly paraphrasing Laura Huxley.

The title of this book is *Something Good for a Change.* If this title is going to work you have to take what lights up for you and turn it into life.

Below you will find a brief list of some of the organizations that have lit up for me in my own personal quest to put my good where it will do the most (for a change).

Now it's your turn. Take what is useful from my list and add on some of your own.

Then go on out and live it!

Amnesty International
322 8th Avenue
New York, N.Y. 10001
212-807-8400

American Friends Service
Committee
1501 Cherry Street
Philadelphia, PA 19102
215-241-7169

Christic Institute
1324 North Capitol Street NW
Washington, D.C. 20002
202-797-8106

International Indian Treaty
Council
710 Layton Street #1
San Francisco, CA 94117
415-566-0251

OxFam America
115 Broadway
Boston, MA 02116
617-482-1211

The Names Project
Box 14573
San Francisco, CA 94114
415-863-5511

Seva Foundation
8 North San Pedro Road
San Raphael, CA 94903
(415) 492-1829
Fax 492-8705

Creating Our Future
High School Environmental
Action
398 South Ferndale
Mill Valley, CA 94941
415-381-6744

Greenpeace USA
1436 U Street NW
Washington, D.C. 20009
202-462-1177

Rainforest Action Network
300 Broadway, Suite 29
San Francisco, CA 94113
414-398-4404

Community for Creative
Non-Violence
425 2nd Street NW
Washington, D.C. 20001-2037
202-393-1909

National Coalition for the
Homeless
1621 Connecticut Avenue NW,
Suite 400
Washington D.C. 20009
202-659-3310

1% for Peace
Box 658
Ithaca, NY 14851
607-273-1919

Plenty International
Box 2306
Davis, CA 95617
916-753-0731